NUDGINGS

NUDGINGS

GENTLE WHISPERS, HOLY REMINDERS

RYAN M. ROBERTS

Nudgings: Gentle Whispers, Holy Reminders

Cover Design by Isaiah Guerrero

ISBN 979-8-9999900-0-6
First Edition

Published by HS Nudgings Press
Boise, Idaho

Printed in the United States of America

For Dina —
my faithful companion and best friend

With joy also for Annie —
our first grandchild, born the year this book came to life

Like grass, we rise with the
morning—yet wither so soon;
long days of summer, too few.

As wildflowers—unexpected,
resplendent, yet fading — we bloom,
beautify, blaze, and then—*poof!*
So good, so brief, so gone.

Nothing lasts. But wait . . .
the love of the Lord churns in the wake
of those who fear Him—
salvation reaching and rippling
to children's children and more.

Your life matters.
Don't toil or spin. Be faithful. Obey.
Love wholly. Live wisely.
Stand forever in Him.

(Psalm 103:15–18; Isaiah 40:8; Luke 12:27)

Contents

Becoming

God in the Ordinary

The Gift of Grace and Gratitude

Christ and the Cross

Called with a Purpose

Hope on the Horizon

INTRODUCTION

The disciples came up and asked, "Why do you tell stories?" He [Jesus] *replied, "You've been given insight into God's kingdom. You know how it works. Not everybody has this gift, this insight; it hasn't been given to them. Whenever someone has a ready heart for this, the insights and understandings flow freely. But if there is no readiness, any trace of receptivity soon disappears. That's why I tell stories: to create readiness, to nudge the people toward a welcome awakening."*
—Matthew 13:10–15, MSG

Have you ever been shoved, bumped, pushed—or nudged?

I've been shoved by a bully on the playground, bumped while carrying a tray of food, and once—quite literally—pushed into an overcrowded subway car in Seoul by a uniformed "pusher" whose job was to cram people in so the doors could close. It was wild… and slightly terrifying.

Those moments left an impression. But none compare to the quiet, soul-shaping power of a gentle nudge from the Holy Spirit. His nudges don't bruise, disrupt, or confine—they awaken the soul.

The Spirit doesn't barge in. He whispers. He woos. He waits. And when He nudges, it's never to condemn or control—it's always to draw us close. To lead us into life. To shape us—moment by moment, breath by breath—into the image of Christ.

God is always nudging—through Scripture, people, prayer, beauty, silence, circumstances, and even pain. He doesn't cause all things, but

He can use anything. What the enemy means for harm, God redeems for good. His voice isn't careless or chaotic—it's persistent, patient, and personal. His nudgings matter. They shape us—if we're willing.

Sometimes it's a verse that won't leave us alone. Other times, it's a question, a phrase, an ache, or a word that cuts through the noise.

We expect thunder, but often He speaks in a whisper. Like Elijah on the mountain, we look for God in the wind, the fire, the earthquake. But more often than not, He comes in a still, small voice.

That's the heart behind this book—not to explain the Spirit's promptings, but to create space where you might discern His gentle nudge.

These reflections came one at a time—week by week, year by year—through ordinary days and sacred moments. They were lived, prayed, wrestled with, written down, and—by God's grace—shared. I've seen the Spirit use them in others, and I pray He'll use them in you.

There's no rigid structure here—no formula or reading plan. Just one thread running through it all—Jesus—the source and sender of every sacred nudge.

In one reflection, you'll read about Paul and Silas singing at midnight—praising from a prison cell. In another, you'll pause and discover why *Commas Matter*. You'll cry out like a child in *Call Out to Jesus*, wrestle with conviction in *A Goad of Grace*, and consider the fleeting nature of time in *Tomorrow Never Comes*. Along the way, you'll reflect on joy, courage, memory, conviction, waiting, wonder—and hope.

This isn't a book about behavior management or spiritual performance. It's about presence—His Presence. It's about a God who is a good teacher and a faithful friend—who meets us where we are, nudges us toward where we need to go, and slowly shapes us into people who reflect Christ's love in the world.

The Apostle Paul once wrote: "*... continue to work out your salvation with fear and trembling, for it is God who works in you to will and to act in order to fulfill his good purpose*" (Philippians 2:12–13, NIV).

That's the mystery and beauty of the Spirit: God is at work within us, nudging us, and we're invited to respond.

Scripture is full of nudges. Sometimes it's a whisper, a dream, a question, a moment of providential timing. The Spirit often makes assignments known, not with a lightning bolt, but with an inner stirring—a holy nudge.

I hope you'll engage with these reflections fully. Read with a pen in hand. Underline what speaks to you. Write in the margins. Dog-ear the pages. Wrestle, rejoice, repent, and respond. Let the Spirit write on your heart. These aren't meant to be skimmed—they're meant to be received.

Lean in. Listen closely. And let these nudgings lift you, like the sycamore tree lifted Zacchaeus—high enough to see Jesus more clearly. To feel His eyes on you. To hear His voice more intimately. And to follow Him more fully.

It's been said that reading a book is like having a conversation with the author. I like that idea. I've always loved meaningful connection—the kind where stories are shared, questions welcomed, and hearts sharpened. I believe in the power of words to encourage and transform. That's what I pray happens here.

May these pages stir something deep—not just thoughts, but prayer. Not just reflection, but response.

May every word nudge you into the gentle, faithful presence of Jesus.

Living with Eternity in View

Tomorrow Never Comes

Today, if you hear his voice, do not harden your hearts…
—Hebrews 3:15, NIV

The other day, I visited a good friend of mine, a wise and godly man who is 91 years old and confined to his bed. I visit him weekly, offering whatever encouragement I can, but it's always me who walks away feeling blessed.

During our time together, I reminded him that today is a unique gift from God, saying, "Today is the only Monday, March 31, 2025, that has ever existed in time and eternity." He paused and replied, "Wow, I guess that's right."

I went on to say, "Yesterday is gone, and tomorrow is uncertain. Today is all we have—it's a gift." My friend smiled knowingly and said, "You know, tomorrow never comes." Then, with a twinkle in his eye, he asked, "Did I ever tell you about the bar in New York?"

I hadn't heard the story, so he shared what I thought was a memory from his younger days. He told me about a bar in New York with a sign on the wall that read, "Free Beer Tomorrow"—where one guy kept coming back every day for his free beer, and the bartender would always say, "Nope, read the sign."

As I chuckled at the old joke, my friend smiled and repeated, "Tomorrow never comes."

And that isn't a joke—it's the truth.

The Enemy deceives us with the illusion of a tomorrow that never comes. He whispers, "There will be time later to get things right. Tomorrow, you'll make that change. Tomorrow, you'll turn to God." But the truth is, tomorrow never arrives. We have "plans" and put things off, thinking, "I'll do it tomorrow." But then we look back months, even years later, and realize all we have is a bunch of empty yesterdays.

Scripture pleads with us: *"Today, if you hear His voice, do not harden your hearts."* Not tomorrow—today. When we hear God's voice—whether it's a gentle nudge to forgive, a prompting to step into something new, or a call to repentance—and we delay, saying, "not yet," we begin to close off the tenderness and trust that a "yes" to God requires. Over time, that repeated "not yet" becomes a hard-hearted "no" without us even realizing it.

God's invitation to "today" isn't for when life settles down or when we feel more ready—it's for now. God is speaking to us in this moment, calling us to surrender, to reconcile, to create, to live fully in Him.

Lean into Jesus. Act now, because… ***tomorrow never comes***.

The Life In Our Hours

Oh! Teach us to live well! Teach us to live wisely and well! … And let the loveliness of our Lord, our God, rest on us, confirming the work that we do. Oh, yes. Affirm the work that we do!
—Psalm 90:12, 17 MSG

The hours of our lives—they are a precious commodity.
We don't want to lose a single one.
So we say to ourselves and to others:
don't smoke,
stay away from fried foods,
exercise regularly,
cut the sugar,
manage your stress,
get regular checkups,
avoid the lines at the DMV,
and, . . . be careful!

We all want to live. We want every hour of life we can get.
Why? So we can watch more Netflix? Football? and Fixer Upper?
Maybe, but too much cotton candy leaves us sick and unsatisfied.
Time flies as hours congeal into days.
Is it time spent or invested?
Do our minutes have meaning?
We give great attention to the hours of our life;
…but what about the life in our hours?

Oh! Teach us to live wisely and well!

It Went So Fast

This moment contains all moments. — C.S. Lewis

"I can't believe I'm graduating in just a few days. It went so fast."

Every spring, these words echo through hallways, campuses, and classrooms. High schoolers say it as they pack up their lockers. College students say it as they finish that last final.

It went so fast? … Really?

Scores of exams, practices, papers, and projects. Years of growing pains, late nights, hard conversations, and last-minute laundry. Every day full—sometimes too full—and yet now, on the edge of what's next, it all feels like a blur.

This is the strange tension of life—long seasons feel short once they're behind us. Moments that once seemed endless now feel like they slipped by in a breath.

We all graduate—from stages, seasons, and versions of ourselves. A toddler becomes a teen. A young couple becomes a family. A home once brimming with laughter and life is now quiet. One day you're in it, and the next you're looking back saying, "It went so fast."

Fast? After all those long nights, hard days, awkward moments, and tearful prayers?

Yes—because when it's over, it all feels like a breath.

The psalmist captures it this way: *"Surely all mankind stands as a mere breath."* (Psalm 39:5, ESV)

A breath is fleeting and often unnoticed—until it's gone. Try holding yours and you'll quickly realize that every single one matters.

That's how life is. Moments rush past, ordinary days pile up, and then suddenly they're behind us—transformed into memory, nostalgia, and the ache of "the good old days."

Andy from *The Office* put it well: *"I wish there was a way to know you're in the good old days before you've actually left them."*

Even Moses, looking back on 120 years filled with calling, adventure, wandering, and walking with God, confessed: *"The years… quickly pass, and we fly away."* (Psalm 90:10, NIV)

And then he prays: *"Teach us to number our days, that we may gain a heart of wisdom."* (Psalm 90:12, NIV)

To "number our days" isn't to count them—it's to live them. To stop long enough to see that today is a gift. To love the people around us. To be awake to the presence and goodness of God in our lives.

Days and breaths are too numerous to count, but both are important. Don't waste them or wish them away. Number them aright—not by counting them, but by making them count.

For you can be sure that the day, the event, the challenge, the goal, the dream—and even the four-year college experience—will be over and done with before you know it. And you'll find yourself saying:

"I can't believe I'm graduating in just a few days. It went so fast."

Whatever Happens

Whatever happens, conduct yourselves in a manner worthy of the gospel of Christ.
—Philippians 1:27, NIV

As I sat in church on Sunday and listened to the sermon, my heart and mind were going in another direction. I saw a guy in church that looked like Rex, the auto shop service advisor that I had interacted with two days earlier. My car had been in for repairs and when I went to pick it up my interaction with Rex was a bit tense. I disagreed with the bill. I had done my research and felt the charges were excessive.

I voiced my concern and made my case convincingly … and a bit curtly. In the end my bill was reduced by $150, but seeing this guy that looked like Rex in church made me think . . . What if it's him? What will he think when he sees me playing bass in the worship band? What will he think of my testimony for the Lord?

As I reflected on my interaction with Rex I concluded that I said and did nothing that was wrong, inappropriate or that I regret, but I still didn't feel right about it. I tried to allay my concern by recalling something I had recently read stating, "Too many of us confuse the words "nice" and "godly." They are not the same thing."

I agree with this. Sometimes hard things need to be said and done and they don't feel and/or appear to be "nice" at the time. I mean c'mon, Jesus flipped tables in the temple, didn't he?

Yes, but He also died upon a cross . . . for me and Rex.

As you can see, as I sat there in church I wasn't listening to the sermon, I was wrestling with things before God. *"Do I just let people run over me? Take advantage of me? Overcharge me? It's not right!"*

Immediately my mind went to a quote from Wayne Dyer that I often repeat to my fifth-grade students, "If you have the choice between being right and being kind, choose being kind."

Then my mind went to Paul's words in Romans 2:4, *"Don't you see how wonderfully kind, tolerant, and patient God is with you? Does this mean nothing to you? Can't you see that his kindness is intended to turn you from your sin?"* (NLT)

Nice? Right? Kind? Godly? I don't necessarily want to be thought of as "nice" but I do want to be "godly"—more specifically—Christlike. What is $150 worth?

In Paul's New Testament letters to the churches he says to make sure that everything you say and do is seasoned with salt so as to present Christ in a tasteful and honorific way in and through your life (Col. 4:6). Jesus is my hope, my help, my Lord and my life. *"I have been crucified with Christ and I no longer live, but Christ lives in me. The life I now live in the body, I live by faith in the Son of God, who loved me and gave himself for me"* (Galatians 2:20, NIV).

God is my provider (Matt. 6:11). He is my portion (Ps. 142:5). He can pay my bills. Do I really need to fight and fuss? Where is my trust? Tyler Staton says that, "Sin is meeting the deep needs of my life by my own resources." When it comes to my needs and immediate concerns ... do I argue, assert myself and exhibit contempt so as to communicate my position, convince my contender and manipulate a situation for my benefit?

Is the $150 discount that transpired after I voiced my concern and complaint worth the uncomfortable conflict and likely diminishment of my testimony for Christ to Rex and the others in the room?
Like I said, in my interaction with Rex, I did and said nothing that was wrong, inappropriate or that I regret, but I still didn't feel right about it. So, at the end of the church service I went up to the guy and asked him if his name was Rex, unfortunately, it wasn't him.

I'm headed back to the auto shop.

Whatever happens…

We Have No Idea

One day as Jesus was walking along the shore of the Sea of Galilee, he saw two brothers—Simon, also called Peter, and Andrew—throwing a net into the water, for they fished for a living. Jesus called out to them, "Come, follow me, and I will show you how to fish for people!" And they left their nets at once and followed him.
—Matthew 4:18-20, NLT

Reading this passage about Peter and Andrew being called by Jesus, my mind immediately goes to two places: the old Yiddish proverb that says, "Man plans, and God laughs," and the children's Sunday School song, "I Will Make You Fishers of Men."

As a child, I would sing that song and cast my imaginary fishing line out into the world, having no idea what a crazy risk it was for Peter and Andrew to follow Jesus. I now realize they probably had life all planned out—grow the business, raise a family, do their best, and enjoy life.

But then Jesus called... and God laughed.

Peter and Andrew had no idea that following Jesus would mean having their lives sung about by children and displayed on flannel graphs throughout the world. They had no idea they would be public speakers, healers, gospel writers, and world-changers. They had no idea they would walk, talk, and partner with the Creator of the Universe—the King of Kings and the Lord of Lords.

We have no idea . . .

Years ago, when our daughters were in elementary school, we bought a home and chose the location carefully. The house was in a nice neighborhood and the nearby junior high and high school were excellent. It was perfect—a good place, good schools, a good plan.

But the year before our oldest child entered junior high, we got an opportunity, took a risk, and moved to South Korea to teach for two years at an international school.

And God laughed.

Neither of my daughters ever went to the junior high and high school in our neighborhood. That two-year stint overseas turned into eight years of new friends, meaningful work and life changing adventure. We all grew deeply in our faith and saw Jesus work in our midst and through our lives in unimaginable ways.

We had no idea.

And now, when I look back and think of my plans versus God's hand of faithfulness in my life—I laugh.

You and I have no idea of all that God wants to do with our lives. We have no idea what He wants to accomplish in and through us today. We have no idea how far His call can carry us.

Follow Jesus.

Delayed, but Not Denied

The Lord's unfailing love surrounds the one who trusts…
—Psalm 32:10, NIV

I once heard a line from a grizzled cowboy in Baker City, Oregon, that's stuck with me—probably because I've lived it: "If you're gonna be dumb, you gotta be tough."

I've done things I regret—and made decisions I wish I could take back. Not because I meant harm, but because I got tired of waiting. Tired of the silence. Tired of nothing moving. Tired of praying and seeing no results.

So I acted. Took things into my own hands. Pushed forward and tried to make something happen. Sometimes we call that "taking charge" or "being courageous." But honestly? It's just forcing what only God can do.

And that's dumb.

Paul knew what that felt like. He got tired of waiting on God. He ignored multiple Spirit-led warnings and pressed ahead to Jerusalem (Acts 21:4, 10–14). His motives weren't impure—but he was stubborn. Impatient. And it caught up with him. He was arrested and ended up stuck in Caesarea for two years under a corrupt governor named Felix (Acts 24:27).

The gospel still burned in his bones. But instead of missionary journeys and new churches, he got silence and stone walls. He was in a holding pattern—no movement, no momentum. Just waiting. And it was his own fault.

But here's the beauty: God didn't write him off. Paul was forgiven. Still loved and still useful. But his path had shifted. He was delayed, but not denied.

This tale echoes another: the Israelites, standing on the edge of the Promised Land. They had just come through the Red Sea, made their way to Sinai—and were only an eleven-day journey from the land God had promised them (Deuteronomy 1:2). But they let fear overrule their faith. They turned back… and spent the next forty years walking in circles (Numbers 14:22–34).

They were so close. But instead of stepping forward in trust—they froze in fear and doubt. And the consequence was a detour they never expected. God forgave them. But the delay still came.

Sometimes that's how it goes. Forgiveness doesn't erase the consequences. But grace never leaves us there. God doesn't walk away. He stays, and He redeems.

So, if you find yourself in a long delay—maybe even one of your own making—don't lose heart. God hasn't benched you. He hasn't given up on you. He still has work for you to do—and grace to carry you through. Even in the wilderness, He can use you. Even behind prison doors, there's hope. And when the waiting ends—and it will—you'll find He was working all along.

There's some real truth in that old line: "If you're gonna be dumb, you gotta be tough." King David knew something about that. But he also knew it wasn't the ultimate truth. He wrote these words after doing something dumb: *"The Lord's unfailing love surrounds the one who trusts in him."* (Psalm 32:10, NIV)

Thankfully, in the Lord, the last word isn't *tough* … it's *trust.*

Trust in Jesus.

What Now?

Or those eighteen who died when the tower in Siloam fell on them—do you think they were more guilty than all the others living in Jerusalem? I tell you, no.
—Luke 13:4–5, NIV

Tragedy happens. We live in a world where car accidents steal lives, wars rage, and society fractures under the weight of conflict. These things grieve us deeply. And yet, in a broken world, where sorrow makes the news every day, we grow used to it—maybe even a little numb.

But then something happens that stops us cold. Something that feels unbearably wrong. Like twenty-seven young lives, taken in an instant—swept away by floodwaters at a church camp. And we're left stunned. Reaching for words. And we find ourselves asking the age-old question: Why?

Jesus once pointed to a tragedy—a tower in Siloam that collapsed and killed eighteen people. The people of His day wanted to understand why. Was it punishment? Did the victims somehow deserve it? Jesus didn't give them an explanation. He gave them an invitation. "Do you think they were worse sinners? I tell you, no. But unless you repent…"

It may sound severe—even insensitive—but what He was doing was gently shifting the question: from *Why?* to *What now?* He was helping them see that tragedy seldom comes with a reason. Yet it always comes with a reminder—life is fragile, and our hope was never meant to rest in this world.

There's a scene in John 11 where Jesus stands at the tomb of His friend Lazarus. He knows resurrection is coming—yet still, He weeps. But before that moment, John tells us that Jesus was "deeply moved." The Greek word used there—*embrimaomai*—means a deep, guttural groaning. Anguish. Rage. Not passive sorrow, but a holy fury—directed at death itself. At the ruin and the sorrow. Because this is not how it was meant to be.

God created a world of love and free choice. He didn't create tragedy. Sin and brokenness did that. And the Enemy has had a heyday with it ever since. But Jesus came to end that reign. That's why He stood at Lazarus' grave. And it's why He willingly walked toward His own. Not to escape death—but to defeat it.

He saw the grief of Mary and Martha. The tower in Siloam. The hospital waiting room. The empty crib. The centuries of names etched in tombstones. And… He saw Camp Mystic.

He went to the cross to undo it all.

The Enemy thought death would finish us. But Jesus walked straight into the grave—and walked out again. Alive. Yet for now, even that doesn't erase the pain. We still grieve. And the question of "why" still haunts us. But we can know this: The One who wept and groaned and raged is redeeming. Jesus is not far off. He is near. He is with us.

So— "what now?" We pray… for those who have lost the ones they love… and for ourselves, that we would hold fast to faith and not be overcome by the temptation to doubt God's goodness.

And we hope and trust in Jesus—the One who will make all things new.

Grace in the Hard Places

Thorns and Nails

They that wait upon the Lord shall renew their strength; they shall mount up with wings as eagles; they shall run, and not be weary; and they shall walk, and not faint.
—Isaiah 40:31, KJV

The other day, I was talking with a friend who had recently undergone a serious heart procedure. Her doctors were monitoring her for three months to determine whether the treatment had been successful. She told me the waiting was the hardest part—every little flutter or twinge sent a wave of concern through her. She looked at me and said, "I'm on pins and needles."

There are moments in life when we wait—when the days stretch on endlessly and uncertainty grips our hearts. We wait for a diagnosis, a job offer—an answer. And in that waiting, we often feel like we're on pins and needles, fraught with anxiety, held captive by the tension of the unknown.

But it doesn't have to be like this. Isaiah 40:31 describes a different kind of waiting: *"They that wait upon the Lord shall renew their strength…"*

In the Bible, the Hebrew word for "wait" conveys the image of interwoven strands—like cords twisted and bound together to form something strong and unbreakable. It's a waiting where our souls are entwined with the Lord's heart rather than tangled in the worry and fear of the world. It's an active, expectant waiting that draws us closer to God's presence and strengthens us with His promises.

Jesus is at the very center of this different kind of waiting. He took on thorns and nails so that you and I wouldn't have to endure pins and needles. He carries us—and the weight of our fears and burdens—so that we might live in peace, no longer captives to anxiety.

Jesus said, *"Peace I leave with you; my peace I give you. I do not give to you as the world gives. Do not let your hearts be troubled and do not be afraid."* (John 14:27, NIV)

He invites us to "wait" upon Him. In Jesus, we soar like eagles, run with strength, and walk without fainting. We are empowered to endure, persevere, and trust, as He is our portion. We trade our pins and needles for His peace—a peace that sustains us in the moment and carries us into the unknown.

It's a peace found in waiting—a waiting He secured for us through thorns and nails.

Deadly Nearness

My Father God, save me from… deadly nearness. – J.H. Jowett

"He came to Jesus at night..." —John 3:2, NIV

Some ironies are tragic. Nicodemus was so near to Jesus, yet so far from Life. We first meet him at night—a Pharisee, a seeker of truth—meeting Jesus under the cover of darkness. Respectful, earnest… yet hesitant.

In John 7, Nicodemus speaks up for Jesus, defending His right to a fair hearing among the Pharisees, and yet he wavers. Reluctant to take a stand—to go all in.

Then, in John 19, Nicodemus helps prepare Jesus' body for burial. He draws near, but Jesus is dead. The call to be born again is missed, and the last time we see him, he stands in the tomb of Jesus—silent.

After this moment, Nicodemus is not heard from again in Scripture. His story fades into history, speculation, and unspoken regret. What could have been is hauntingly gone. This is the sound of deadly nearness—a stillness that follows a life lived just outside the fullness of faith.

It's more than a missed opportunity; it's a choice—a failure to embrace the life that Jesus offers. The truth and presence of Christ are right in front of us, but we hold back, preferring our misery over His mystery. All that remains is a silent void—a deadly nearness.

Some ironies are truly tragic.

Dear Jesus, save me from deadly nearness. May I not linger in the shadows, hesitating at the threshold of Your love and grace. Help me lean fully into You, embracing the Life and transformation that You offer. Teach me to live my faith boldly, and walk with You in Spirit and in Truth. Amen.

A Mess

For the joy set before him [Jesus] *endured the cross, scorning its shame, and sat down at the right hand of the throne of God.*
—Hebrews 12:2, NIV

The joy set before Jesus was you and me! He went through the horrific pain, struggle and humiliation of the cross so we could find mercy, grace and life with God.

When I was 27 years old I left my job as a fifth-grade teacher and took a position as an elementary school principal. That might sound good and glorious, but it was difficult ... I mean—diarrhea every day—difficult.

I was the youngest adult in the building, I was the boss, and I was a nervous wreck. One day I was so stressed that when the secretary brought a purchase order into my office for me to sign, all I could do was scribble—and it looked nothing like my signature. The secretary saw my shaky hand and with concern said, "Oh Ryan..."

I was a mess.

At the time, being a principal wasn't my dream job, but it paid the bills (nearly double what I made as a teacher) and made it possible for my wife to stay home and care for our newborn daughter. I didn't like the stress and the struggle, but that didn't matter. I was thankful for the job and did it for the joy set before me—my wife and my daughter. But all that doesn't come close to what Jesus did for you and for me.

He left Heaven, came to earth as a baby, lived as a servant, healed the sick, loved the unlovely and showed us God's heart. And in return, He was wrongly accused, slapped, spit upon, mocked, beaten and tortured. He was stripped naked, impaled on a wooden cross and died a criminal's death.

He could have called ten-thousand angels and stopped the pain and injustice, but He didn't. He did the hard thing. He paid the price for you, me and the whole world, so that we might be free from the power of sin and death in our lives. We were a mess, but while we were yet sinners, Christ died for us.

He did it for the joy set before Him and that joy was you and me!

Singing at Midnight

About midnight, Paul and Silas were praying and singing hymns to God, and the other prisoners were listening to them.
—Acts 16:25, NIV

Is there any darker moment than the "midnight hour"? The silence is suffocating, the path unclear, and hope is all but gone. It's the hour of waiting—when nothing changes, when prayers feel unanswered, and when suffering simply lingers.

Yet, in Acts 16:25, we find Paul and Silas—wounded, bound, and waiting. And what are they doing?

They're singing.

Not because their chains had fallen off. Not because morning had come. But because Christ was with them in the dark. Their joy wasn't tied to release or relief—it was rooted in the presence of the One who never leaves. That's the kind of joy the way of Jesus calls us to—a joy that does not deny suffering but sings through it.

I have heard that song before.

One of the greatest privileges of my life was spending four spring breaks at a children's home in Bangalore, India. The children there had very little—simple meals, few possessions, no shoes—but their hearts overflowed with the love, joy, and peace of Jesus. Each evening, we gathered for worship, and oh how they could sing! Their voices rang out—strong, unwavering, full of faith.

Electricity there was rationed, and at some point each night, the lights would flicker and fail, plunging us into thick darkness. But the singing never faltered. If anything, it soared. There was no hesitation. Just voices rising and ringing out, cutting through the night with unshaken praise.

Then, from the shadows, a child would speak: "The Lord is my light and my salvation—whom shall I fear?" Another voice would follow: "They that wait upon the Lord shall renew their strength." Then another, and another. Scripture wove through the dark like a golden thread, stitching faith into the night.

Years later, I can still hear their singing. It's a melody of faith that lingers in my soul.

The Christian life isn't about avoiding the shadows. It's about walking through them with Jesus, the Light of the world. When we trust in His presence we find the strength to rejoice—not because life is easy, but because He is near.

At midnight, Paul and Silas sang. The prisoners listened. So did the guards. And now, centuries later, we do too.

Faith in the darkness isn't just for us—it's a testimony to the world around us. Will we be people who sing at midnight? Will we walk the way of Jesus—joyful, fearless, and trusting that He is greater than anything we face?

Whether it's midnight or midday, no light shines brighter than Jesus. When the lights go out and the darkness falls—sing! Let the melody of your hope shine forth, because someone is always listening.

A Goad of Grace

When the blood of your martyr Stephen was shed, I stood there giving my approval and guarding the clothes of those who were killing him.
—Acts 22:20, NIV

There's that one thing.

You know what it is—and I do too. The moment you wish you could rewrite. That thing you did—or stood by and let happen. Sometimes it haunts us. Other times, we almost forget—tucking it under the pile of "good" we've done. Time and distance help us rationalize it and we move on... sort of.

But then comes the poke. A word. A memory. A moment that left a mark. And we feel it—deeply. It presses and prods. It won't let you stay where you are.

That's what a goad does.

Goad is not a word we use much anymore, but in the ancient world, it was a pointed stick used by a farmer to prod an ox in the right direction. If the animal resisted—if it kicked back—it only ended up hurting itself more.

That's the image Jesus used when He addressed Saul on the road to Damascus: *"Saul, Saul, why are you persecuting me? It is hard for you to kick against the goads."* (Acts 26:14, ESV)

Goads aren't just painful—they're persistent. They dig, prod, and poke. They're not meant to destroy—but to guide. You know that sting of conviction? That holy discomfort that won't leave you alone? It might not be punishment—it just might be a goad of grace.

For Saul, I wonder if one of those goads was the face of Stephen—the first Christian martyr. Saul was there when he died—approving of his murder. But Stephen didn't curse. Instead, he forgave. He looked up to heaven and prayed for the very ones throwing the stones.

That kind of love leaves a mark.

Maybe that image was seared into Saul's mind. Maybe it played on repeat in his soul. Here's the truth: God doesn't waste anything—not even our worst moments. The very thing the Enemy meant to use as shame, God can use as a holy irritation, a divine haunting—a goad—not to condemn, but to call us closer.

Jesus didn't die on the cross to let our past have the last word. He's holy—and the pain and guilt we carry didn't come from Him. But in His mercy, He takes it on and transforms it. He loves us with a relentless love, and that nudge in your spirit, that ache of regret, that tension you can't shake—it's not an interruption. It's an invitation.

He goads us—not to shame us, but to save us. Not to punish, but to pursue. Until we find our peace in Him we'll keep feeling unsettled—not because He's far off, but because He's drawing near. Pressing in. His grace won't let us go.

That's what happened to Saul. The goads became grace. The one who tried to silence the church became Paul—the gospel's most passionate preacher.

Sometimes the most merciful thing God can do is make us uncomfortable. His loving conviction might feel like a sharp prod in the ribs, but it's actually His kindness—leading us to repentance (Romans 2:4).

So, if something's poking at you, don't kick against it. Don't run away. Lean in—and listen to Jesus.

It might just be a goad of grace.

Trust Beyond Trace

Your road led through the sea, your pathway through the mighty waters—a pathway no one knew was there!
—Psalm 77:19, NLT

In the year 155, Polycarp, the elderly pastor of Smyrna, was dragged into a Roman arena. He had been discipled by the apostle John, and he had known people who had seen the risen Christ with their own eyes. The governor pressed him to deny Jesus and swear by Caesar. Polycarp's reply was calm and unshakable: "Eighty and six years I have served Him, and He has done me no wrong. How then can I blaspheme my King who saved me?"

His sentence was death by fire. They tied him to a stake and lit the wood. Witnesses said the flames arched around him like the sail of a great ship, refusing to consume him. When the fire would not finish the task, a blade was thrust into his side (sound familiar?).

From the outside, it looked like the end. A faithful life brought to a violent close. But Polycarp knew better. His faith was exactly what Hebrews 11:1 describes: *being sure of what we hope for and confident in what we do not see.* Death itself was not the end—it was a doorway into the presence of Christ.

This is how God works. In the Old Testament, it was through the sea. Israel stood trapped, water before them, Pharaoh's chariots behind. Fear screamed that the way was closed. But then God's breath split the waters and revealed dry ground—a pathway no one knew was there.

In the New Testament, it was through the cross. To the disciples, it looked like finality—Jesus crucified, hope buried, everything lost. Rome's instrument of shame was meant to silence the movement once for all. But God turned that place of death into the very road to salvation. From the cross came forgiveness, resurrection, and life. A pathway no one imagined.

Henry Law once wrote, "It is our wisdom to trust when we have no skill to trace." Isn't that where faith lives? When God's footprints aren't visible. When your map runs out. When decline or disappointment whisper that the road is over. We simply must trust.

When there seems to be no way, Jesus is the way. God's path may be hidden until the very moment you need it, but it is never absent. Sometimes it's found in the next prayer, the next act of obedience, the next breath of trust.

The noise of fear is loud. It's the clatter of Pharaoh's chariots. The roar of the Roman crowd. The steady ticking clock of time reminding us of our own mortality. But greater still is the presence of the Lord, who rides across the skies, who makes roads through seas, brings victory through a cross, and life through death.

Now faith is confidence in what we hope for and assurance about what we do not see (Hebrews 11:1, NIV).

In Jesus—we trust beyond trace.

He… is the Pathway.

Why?

For this is how God loved the world: He gave his one and only Son, so that everyone who believes in him will not perish but have eternal life.
—John 3:16, NLT

I will never forget the advice I received from a wise mentor about handling tough situations and navigating challenging interactions in life. He said, "Don't get hung up on what is said, but instead, look a little deeper and consider: why is it being said?"

That thought, *"why is it being said?"* came to mind as I considered the Christmas story this year. In the account of Jesus' birth, there were wise men from the east that travelled to Bethlehem to find the newborn king of the Jews, and when they found Him, *"They entered the house and saw the child with his mother, Mary, and they bowed down and worshiped him. Then they opened their treasure chests and gave him gifts of gold, frankincense, and myrrh."* (Matthew 2:11, NLT)

Academic circles abound with controversy, debate, and skepticism concerning the specifics of the wise men in the Christmas story (were there really three?). In the Gospel of Matthew, it says that magi from the east saw a star and discerned the coming of a great king. They sought out the mystery, interacted with the infamous King Herod, and eventually found the child. The Scriptures say the magi brought the newborn king gifts. There is a wealth of jokes and puns surrounding the tale of the wise men and their offerings, but beyond all the debates and jest, I found myself looking a little deeper and asking, "Why did God tell us about the wise men and their gifts?"

The gifts the magi brought to Jesus were unique, glorious and mysterious—full of foreshadowing and promise. The first gift mentioned was gold. Gold was the most costly and precious metal of the day and was equated with royalty. It was an extravagant gift—steeped in sacrifice. The gold of the magi tells the world that the baby Jesus is a royal king—*the King, to Whom every knee will bow, in heaven and on earth and under the earth* (Phil. 2:10, NLT).

The second gift from the magi was frankincense, an aromatic resin made from tree bark. In the Old Testament, dried frankincense was a part of the temple candles that were used in the Holy of Holies. The sweet fragrance of incense, rising up from those candles, symbolized prayer and the Spirit within that Holy Place. The gift of frankincense, given to the baby Jesus, highlights his role as our great high Priest—interceding for us all at the throne of grace (Heb. 4:16, ESV).

The magi's final gift, myrrh, must have left Mary and Joseph scratching their heads, because the ancients used myrrh to embalm dead bodies. The birth of Jesus was about life, not death, … wasn't it? The angel said, *"I bring you good news of great joy that will be for all the people. For unto you is born this day in the city of David a Savior, who is Christ the Lord"* (Luke 2:10-11, ESV).

God sent baby Jesus into the world to save us—and this is where the symbolism of myrrh becomes apparent—Jesus saved us through his suffering and death on a cruel Roman cross. He came as a baby to die for you and me.

So, as you reflect on the Christmas story, be sure to look closely. Don't get hung up on the words, but instead ask about the "why."

Consider the baby Jesus as royal King, great High Priest, and our sacrificial Savior, and then look even deeper . . . into the depths of God's love for you (John 3:16).

His Address Is Grace

You're blessed when you're at the end of your rope.
—Matthew 5:3, MSG

Some time ago, I was diagnosed with a rare, deadly disease—one that only five in a million people get. It was a tumor called an insulinoma, hidden deep in my pancreas. And it was killing me. For six long months, I went from doctor to doctor with no answers. My symptoms worsened, and my strength faded. I was scared, frustrated, and desperate—clinging to Jesus. I was in a tight spot. But while I was there, something deeper was happening.

King David once prayed, *"O God of my righteousness: Thou hast enlarged me when I was in distress."* (Psalm 4:1, KJV)

King David was in a tight space—and God met him with wide grace. Not just by providing escape, but by expanding his heart. God made room—for trust to deepen, for love to grow, and for David to glimpse the height, depth, width, and length of His presence. Like David, I found that when the Lord steps into our distress, freedom and hope follow—even in the tightest places.

I ended up making three trips to the Mayo Clinic in Minnesota. Through the skill of the medical team—and by the grace of God—the tumor was found and removed. I was healed. But even more miraculous than the healing… I was changed. Not just in body—but in soul.

Dallas Willard once said, "God's address is at the end of your rope." Some have suggested that if that truth had a website, it might be called:

www.attheendofyourrope.com. It's not a real URL, of course—but the metaphor holds. It's where striving ends… and grace begins. And I was unquestionably there—at the end of my rope. I had nothing left but God… and the faithful prayers of my friends, family, and church.

Not only was I in a tight place—but I felt completely alone. A bit like Jonah. Trapped in the belly of a whale. Isolated. Powerless. Waiting. And it was there, in that dark, hidden place, that prayer and faith became real. To tie in with the earlier URL reference, here's a fitting hashtag for my Instagram friends: *#inthebellyofawhale.* It's where faith is born—and where prayer gets honest.

Eugene Peterson once noted that in parts of Eastern Europe, some pulpits were built in the shape of a whale. To preach, the pastor had to ascend through the belly and speak from the mouth. It wasn't just a clever design. It was a deep conviction: something happens in a tight place that can't happen anywhere else. The belly of the whale is a place of reckoning and surrender. It's where dead hearts find clarity—and new life begins.

The journey you're in now? That rope? That belly? They're not detours. They're not too much for God. And they're not signs He's forgotten you. They're the very places of transformation—the places where grace finds us.

Here's the invitation Jesus offers to anyone in that place: *"Come to me, all you who are weary and burdened…"* (Matthew 11:28).

So whether you're barely hanging on at *www.attheendofyourrope.com*, or gasping for breath at *#inthebellyofawhale*… remember: you're not lost. You're not alone. Jesus is already there. Look to Him.

His address… is grace.

Scars Tell a Story

I went to the dermatologist the other day for a full-body checkup and the doctor pointed at the five scars on my stomach and said, "I bet there's a story there." I could have shared with him a long, detailed account about sickness, struggle, fear, frustration, doubt, tears, disappointment, long nights, prayers, miracles and praise, but I didn't. I just responded, "Yep, those scars are from the pancreatic surgery I had a couple of years ago at the Mayo Clinic. That surgery saved my life."

Scars tell a story. Jesus had scars on his hands and feet from being hung on a cross for you and for me, and those scars speak volumes ... and they are still speaking today. They tell a story of presence, peace, healing, power and love.

Three days after his crucifixion some of Jesus' disciples were walking to the town of Emmaus when they encountered another traveler. They walked and talked with the stranger for hours, but they didn't know who he was until they saw the nail prints on his hands and, *"then their eyes were opened and they recognized him."* When they saw the scars, they knew it was Jesus (see Luke 24:30-31).

Later that same day, in the city of Jerusalem, Jesus appeared to a gathering of disciples through barred gates and locked doors, but his presence and words of comfort had no calming effect upon them. The face they saw looked vaguely familiar, but not enough to distinguish him from the other men in that region. The disciples were tentative, frightened and doubting, but then Jesus showed them the marks on his hands and feet and then they knew it was him. He was known to them by his scars (see Luke 24:36-39).

Decades later, long after the crucifixion and resurrection of Jesus, the Apostle John was given a glimpse into Heaven where he saw a prophetic and symbolic scene from the gathering of all gatherings. The one who is the King of Kings, Lord of Lords and Creator of the Universe was being called upon to victoriously open the scrolls of all time and eternity, and John, along with billions of others in the crowd, was scanning the stage, eagerly looking for the Lion of the tribe of Judah—the only One worthy of opening the scrolls——but He was nowhere to be found.

Instead, at the center of it all, stood a lamb that looked as if it had been slaughtered. The sacrificial lamb was Jesus, bearing the scars of His crucifixion (see Revelation 5:6).

Scars tell a story, and the scars of Jesus are still speaking today. The story they tell is all about you and me. The Apostle Peter writes, "*Jesus personally carried our sins in his body on the cross so that we can be dead to sin and live for what is right. By his wounds you are healed*" (1 Peter 2:24, NLT).

If you ask me about the scars of Jesus, there's definitely a story there

. . . those scars saved my soul and my life.

Choosing to Trust

Seemingly Impossible

Your road led through the sea, your pathway through the mighty waters—a pathway no one knew was there!
—Psalm 77:19, NLT

On the day that marked the fifth anniversary of my healing from a life-threatening pancreatic tumor, I found myself reflecting on memories nuanced with words like: rare, unknown, insulinoma, failed attempts, trouble, doubt, impossible, Mayo Clinic, suffering, faith, prayer, help… and God.

As I sat there, healthy and thankful, I thought of Psalm 77 and its tale of the sea, the mighty waters, and the hidden pathway I didn't know was there. My story (and yours) is part of God's greater story.

When the children of Israel followed God's direction away from the Egyptian army, they suddenly faced a seemingly impossible obstacle—the Red Sea. From their vantage point, it was hopeless. No escape. No salvation. Their path with God had led them to a dead-end… or so it seemed.

But the story didn't end there. God parted the sea, making a way no one could have imagined. He delivered His people and destroyed their enemies.

God made a way where there seemed to be no way.

The same God that made a way for the Israelites thousands of years ago came to earth in His Son, Jesus Christ. He died on the cross to give us life. God loves us that much! Jesus is the "way," the truth and the life (John 14:6, NIV).

What challenges are you facing today—illness, personal struggles, global crises, overwhelming doubt? We're constantly surrounded by reminders of hopelessness. But remember: God is not limited by what we perceive as reality. He led the children of Israel down a pathway that no one knew was there—no one except God.

Are you up against a seemingly impossible situation? Be encouraged: God knows... and He knows the way through.

Call upon and trust in Jesus—He is the God who makes a way.

Surviving, But… Thirsty

On the last day, the climax of the festival, Jesus shouted to the crowds: "If anyone is thirsty, let him come to me and drink. For the Scriptures declare that rivers of living water shall flow from the inmost being of anyone who believes in me."
—John 7:37–38, TLB

Life has a way of running us dry. Some days are exhilarating, others exhausting, and often both at once. We push through, we keep going, but underneath it all—we're thirsty.

Thirst is a signal, a reminder that the body needs water. Ignore it long enough, and the consequences are serious. The same is true for trees. When trees lack water, they can hang on for a while, but they become vulnerable to the devastating effects of beetles. Beetles thrive on trees that aren't adequately watered. But a well-watered tree produces an abundance of sap—so much that when a beetle bores in, the sap overflows and drowns it. The tree's health and protection come from its access to water. Without it, survival gives way to decline.

That's a picture of our spiritual lives. Without the living water of Jesus, we may manage for a while, but we become vulnerable to the Enemy's schemes and the slow creep of spiritual decay. But when we are well-watered in Christ, He produces such abundant life within us that the Enemy's attacks can't hold. Our strength and protection come from Him alone.

The invitation still stands:

"Is anyone thirsty? Come and drink…" (Isaiah 55:1, NLT).

"Those who drink the water I give will never be thirsty again. It becomes a fresh, bubbling spring within them, giving them eternal life" (John 4:14, NLT).

You don't have to settle for surviving. Jesus offers living water—enough to quench your thirst, guard your heart, and overflow into life. Come to the source. Drink deeply.

Let Him fill you… until you thrive and flourish.

Clinging

"Don't cling to me," Jesus said, "for I haven't yet ascended to the Father. But go find my brothers and tell them, 'I am ascending to my Father and your Father, to my God and your God.'"
—John 20:17, NLT

When I think of clinging, my mind goes to Bangalore, India.

It was my privilege to work at an international school in South Korea for eight years, and a part of the school's educational program included service to others. During Spring Break each year the school would send students out on service trips throughout Asia, and for four of those years it was my pleasure to lead a team of high school students to an orphanage in Bangalore.

What a joy it was for me and my family to spend time with the precious children there in that place. It was a week filled with talking, playing, teaching, singing, laughing, loving and making new friends. From those times and experiences, I carry a myriad of rich memories, but the one that stands out the most is the way the little ones would cling to me when I was holding them.

There were scores of children in that place and they all wanted to be picked up, held and carried around—and they didn't want to be put down. They clung tightly as I held them in my arms. They loved the time and attention—and I loved them.

When we're desperate—we cling just like Mary did on that first Easter morning when she saw Jesus alive near the empty tomb. She was clinging to him and He said to her, "Don't cling to me for I haven't yet ascended to the Father."

But today, Jesus is available to you, me, and the entire world. He has ascended to heaven and has sent His Spirit to live in and among us. He wants us to cling to Him.

Cling tightly to the Lord your God. (Joshua 23:8, NLT)

Cling to your faith in Christ, and keep your conscience clear. (1 Timothy 1:19, NLT)

[O God] *my soul clings to you; your right hand upholds me.* (Psalm 63:8, ESV)

Jesus said, "I tell you the truth, unless you turn from your sins and become like little children, you will never get into the Kingdom of Heaven." (Matthew 18:3, NLT)

Jesus is alive and he is as close as the mention of his name. He has you in His arms and He won't put you down. He loves you.

It's OK... Cling to Jesus.

Call Out to Jesus

The LORD is near to all who call on him.
—Psalm 145:18, NIV

I'll never forget the day my daughter Becca broke her arm.

We were at the elementary school playground near our house. She was in first grade—full of energy and confidence—climbing on the monkey bars and calling out, "Watch this, Daddy!" I was close by, watching and "oohing" and "aahing." Then it happened.

Becca slipped off the bars and fell to the ground. Instinctively, she put her hand out to break her fall and landed on her arm. As I ran toward her, she looked up and cried, "Daddy!" I can still hear her voice—shaky, scared, and full of pain. It pierced my heart.

I helped her immediately. I gently cradled her hurt arm in my hands and calmly told her that everything was going to be OK. I held her close as we walked home and assured her that her mom and I were going to take her to the doctor. Two hours later, Becca's tears and pain were replaced with a good story and a fancy blue cast—and I was the first person to sign it.

"Daddy!" ... I'll never forget the sound of her cry. Even before she called out to me, I was running to help—because I love her. How much more does our Father in heaven love us?

He longs for us to call out to Him—and a cry is all it takes. When it comes to prayer, God isn't picky. He wants to hear from us and help us, because He loves and delights in us—just like a parent delights in their child.

The instinct to cry out to God isn't just a child's response on a playground—it has been a part of the human story since Genesis.

"To Seth also a son was born, and he called his name Enosh. At that time people began to call upon the name of the LORD*."* (Genesis 4:26, ESV)

To "call on the name of the Lord" means to cry out—to place your hope and trust in Him. This is the first moment in Scripture where people began to pray—really pray. And here's what's remarkable: Seth's line leads all the way to Jesus.

Seth was Adam and Eve's third son (remember the whole Cain and Abel situation?). And it was through Seth's lineage—the one where people first began to call on the Lord—that God would one day send the Savior. Genesis 5 traces that line: from Seth to Noah, then to Abraham, David… and finally to Jesus (Luke 3:38).

Jesus is both the fulfillment of prayer and the one who makes it possible. Prayer began in His lineage—and through His life, death, and resurrection Jesus opened the way for all of us to call upon God freely, confidently, and without shame. There is no access to the Father apart from Him. He's the reason our prayers are heard. He is the way to the One we cry out to.

When we pray—when we call on the name of the Lord—we're not just speaking into the air. We're stepping into a story that began in Genesis and finds its fulfillment in Jesus.

So don't hold back. Whether it's a shout of faith or a whisper of desperation—He hears you. And He's already running toward you.

Call out to Jesus.

Are You Thirsty?

As the deer pants for streams of water, so my soul pants for you, my God. My soul thirsts for God, for the living God.
—Psalm 42:1-2, NIV

Are you thirsty? In 1985, I went on a college choir tour to Europe in the month of July. The weather was hot and humid and all of us in the choir were a sweaty mess—and constantly thirsty. The director kept warning us, "Don't drink the public water!" because it wasn't safe. Disposable water bottles weren't common yet (it was the '80s) and clean water was hard to come by. We had to rely on purified water from the markets and restaurants that we encountered while touring by bus. Between that, and the relentless heat, … I was really thirsty.

Eventually, my thirst won out. At one point in the trip, we were in a small shopping mall in Germany and I went into the public restroom, turned on the sink, and let the water run for a while. It looked fine. I cupped my hands under the flow, and took a long drink. It tasted great, and my thirst was quenched, ... for the moment.

After the trip, I returned home with a camera full of photos, lots of great memories, and a sick stomach—I was losing weight, dealing with diarrhea, and felt lousy. I tried to wait it out, hoping it would go away, but it didn't. Eventually, my parents insisted I see a doctor.

After a thorough examination and a blood test, nothing unusual showed up. The doctor was stumped. He asked, "Have you been camping recently? Is there any chance you might have come into contact with contaminated water?"

I thought for a moment, and then it hit me—Germany! I told him that I had gotten really thirsty and drank from a public faucet in a German shopping mall. The doctor immediately diagnosed me with Giardia, prescribed some medicine, and within a few weeks, I was cured.

Are you thirsty? Of course you are—we all are. But it's a thirst that water can't quench. It's an empty longing we often try to satisfy with binge-watching, endless scrolling, late-night snacks, an extra scoop of ice cream, impulse buying, and lots of other things that are much more costly and damaging than Giardia. The "mall" of the world looks good to our thirsty hearts and minds, but offers up "bad" water—leaving us sick and unsatisfied.

But there is hope and help for our parched souls, and his name is Jesus.

Jesus said, *"Let anyone who is thirsty come to me and drink. …whoever drinks the water I give them will never thirst. Indeed, the water I give them will become in them a spring of water welling up to eternal life. … Come! Let the one who is thirsty come; and let the one who wishes take the free gift of the water of life."* (John 7:37; John 4:14; Rev. 22:17, NIV)

Jesus is the answer to our deepest thirst. He isn't just a temporary fix—He's the source that truly satisfies. In Him, we find the abundant life we crave.

Don't settle for anything less. Drink deeply from His well of goodness, grace, and love today.

Are you thirsty? … Look to Jesus.

Don’t

Have you noticed all the “don’ts” in Ephesians 4?

> Don't be rebellious,
> don't lie,
> don't pretend to be something you're not,
> don't seek revenge,
> don't stay angry,
> don’t drive angry,
> *(sorry, that's not from Eph. 4, it's from the movie, “Groundhog Day”)*
> don't steal,
> don't use foul language,
> don't talk bad about people,
> and don't hold a grudge.

All of those "don'ts" are good advice, but they pale in comparison to the "don'ts" in Ephesians 4:30:

“Don’t grieve God. Don’t break his heart. His Holy Spirit, moving and breathing in you, is the most intimate part of your life, making you fit for himself. Don’t take such a gift for granted.” (MSG)

Wow, maybe you should read that again . . .

God is not a cosmic killjoy, He is joy. Jesus came to give us life—His life—moving, breathing and living in us. We were made to have the Spirit of God filling and empowering our lives, and anything less simply breaks the heart of God.

The "don'ts" of Ephesians 4 aren't there to keep us in line, they are there to keep us in Him. His Holy Spirit is a precious gift.

So, as we walk into another day full of challenges, trials, and temptations, and are faced with the choice to dabble in or do something that will be detrimental to the most intimate part of our life, let's all take Paul's advice—

Don't.

I Choose Jesus

Normally it takes only eleven days to travel from Mount Sinai to Kadesh-barnea, going by way of Mount Seir. But forty years after the Israelites left Egypt, on the first day of the eleventh month, Moses addressed the people of Israel.
—Deuteronomy 1:2–3, NLT

I was somewhere on the border of Idaho and Washington—basically in the middle of nowhere. Cruising along with the windows down, music playing, in the zone (read: not paying attention) … and I missed my exit.

And not by a little.

This wasn't an "Oops, I'll just turn around at the next block" kind of miss. No—this was one of those remote stretches of freeway where the next crossover is miles down the road. So, I kept driving… and driving… and driving. Finally, I found an offramp where I could get to the other side, backtrack, and find my way again. By the time I got back on course, I'd added nearly 90 minutes to my trip.

That kind of detour leaves a mark.

But here's the thing—my little detour was nothing compared to the one the Israelites took. They were headed from Egypt to the Promised Land, a trip that, on paper, should've taken eleven days. But in reality? It took them forty years.

They spent forty years on a journey that should've lasted eleven days.

And the crazy thing? It wasn't the distance or the difficulty that delayed them—it was the path they chose to take.

My excuse for missing the freeway exit that day was simple: I was listening to music and not paying attention to the signs. But what were the Israelites doing (or not doing) that delayed them by forty years?

I found the answer in Psalm 78. It says that God rescued the Israelites from bondage and slavery in Egypt, saved them from Pharaoh's army by parting the Red Sea, guided them by cloud and by fire, gave them water to drink and food to eat (which is essentially saying that God gave them life)—and yet… they kept on sinning. They failed to trust God. They complained, they rebelled, and they did not remember Him, His ways, or His presence in their lives.

They spent forty years on a journey that should have lasted eleven days—because of worry, grumbling, whining, a bad attitude, an ungrateful spirit, and… sin.

Now that's an exit you don't want to take. It'll lead you down a road that strips you of hope, leaves you with regret, and robs you of precious years—even entire seasons—of your life.

I don't know about you, but I don't want to lose 90 minutes of time, let alone 40 years. And I doubt Moses and the Israelites did either. Most of the folks who started that eleven-day journey never made it, and forty years later, they were gone.

Not everyone missed the exit, though. Joshua made it—and his words are worth listening to: *"Choose today whom you will serve… As for me and my family, we will serve the LORD"* (Joshua 24:15, NLT).

To choose Jesus is to walk with Him—daily. It means letting go of the grumbling spirit, the fearful heart, the clenched fist that says, "I know better." It's a posture of trust, even when the road ahead is unclear. It's choosing gratitude over complaint, faith over fear, and obedience—not just when it's easy, but because He's Lord.

Forty years or eleven days…

You choose.

Press On

I came to you in weakness with great fear and trembling.
—1 Corinthians 2:3, NIV

Recently, I went on a five-day backpacking trip that ended with a brutal 15-mile hike out. The first three miles were straight down—no trail, just loose rock, fallen trees, boulder fields, and steep terrain that punished with every step. By the bottom, my legs felt like Jell-O. Then came twelve more miles on a long, winding path that seemed like it would never end. Forty pounds on my back. Blisters on my feet. And somewhere along the way, I hit my limit.

The voice in my head was shouting: "This is impossible. I can't take another step. Everything hurts. … Help!" But I had to keep going. I wasn't alone—I was with five others. We had miles to go, and we were in it together. There was no shortcut and no option to tap out. The only way home… was forward.

Ever had one of those moments? Not just on a trail—but in life? When the loss you never saw coming hits harder than you imagined. When the job falls through. When the diagnosis returns. When your kids drift from the faith. When the dream goes unrealized. When you're older than you used to be—and not where you thought you'd be. When the weight of simply keeping going feels like too much.

You're not alone.

Paul knew that feeling. He left Athens, where his message had mostly fallen flat, and made his way to Corinth—one of the darkest, most spiritually resistant cities in the Roman world. By the time he arrived, he was completely spent. He didn't fake strength. He said, "I came to you in weakness, with great fear and trembling."

That wasn't exaggeration. It was honesty. And even in that place of weakness, the gospel was still at work. People were listening. Lives were being changed. And yet... resistance continued.

Challenge and struggle don't always come with drama. Sometimes they arrive as a slow, steady grind. A quiet voice that whispers, "This isn't making a difference." A heaviness that settles in and won't let go. An ache in the silence when you pray. A moment when you start to wonder if faithfulness is even worth it.

Paul experienced this. But he didn't quit. That's why I hold onto his words from prison: *"I press on toward the goal..."* (Philippians 3:14, NIV). It's not about pushing harder—it's about not giving up. It's not about having all the answers—it's about holding onto Jesus, who is the answer.

That phrase—*press on*—has become a kind of sacred rhythm in my life. It's something I say to others as they move through life with all its joys and challenges. It's how I often close conversations, letters, and emails—not as a cliché, but as an intentional encouragement. A quiet admonition to keep going, keep trusting, and keep walking with Jesus.

In a fragile moment, Jesus spoke to Paul: *"Do not be afraid... for I am with you"* (Acts 18:9–10). Paul's fear didn't disqualify him—it drew God near. God didn't say, "Get over it." Or, "Just do it." He said, "I'm here. Keep going."

And He says the same to you and me.

So wherever you are—however heavy the pack feels, or how long the road seems—look to Jesus ... and ***press on***.

Keep Seeking Him

The Lord passed in front of Moses, calling out, "Yahweh! The Lord! The God of compassion and mercy! I am slow to anger and filled with unfailing love and faithfulness. I lavish unfailing love to a thousand generations. I forgive iniquity, rebellion, and sin."
—Exodus 34:6–7, NLT

Have you ever read something in the Bible that didn't sit right?

A friend of mine recently did. He's sincerely seeking the Lord and told me he's reading through the entire Bible for the first time. As we talked, I watched his face grow serious. He was reading the Word to be inspired—but instead, he ran into something that unsettled him—something that made him flinch.

"Why would God command the Israelites to destroy entire cities when they entered the Promised Land?" he asked. "Honestly, it feels... harsh."

Maybe you've felt that too. You come across something in Scripture—or in life—that doesn't line up with the God you thought you knew. And in those moments, it's easy to define God by what you don't understand. But that's exactly when you need to keep seeking—and remember what He says about Himself.

When God introduced Himself to Moses, He didn't lead with a title or a resume. He revealed His very nature: *"The God of compassion and mercy! I am slow to anger and filled with unfailing love and faithfulness."*

This wasn't a passing comment. It was a defining declaration. He is mercy, love, and faithfulness. And that thread runs through the whole story of Scripture—proclaimed by the prophets, embodied in Jesus, and poured out on the cross.

The destruction of sin has never been arbitrary. It's holy, just, necessary... and bloody. The same God who commanded judgment in Canaan bore that judgment on a cross at Calvary. He didn't overlook evil—He confronted it, and then took it upon Himself.

The cross stands outside of time, and from it God's mercy flows forward into the future and backward into the past—even into the stories we still struggle to understand. His methods may vary—and sometimes confuse us—but His mission of love and mercy never changes.

Just ask Elijah.

In 1 Kings 19, the prophet Elijah was exhausted and afraid, hiding in a cave. Then God said, *"Go out and stand on the mountain, for the Lord is about to pass by."*

Elijah braced himself. He knew the stories—the ways God had shown up before: in a whirlwind, an earthquake, and in the burning bush. So he waited. The wind howled, the earth shook, and the fire blazed. But God was in none of it.

Then came a whisper. God hadn't changed. He showed up in a way Elijah didn't expect—not with spectacle, but with stillness. No matter the context, God's character is the same. He's still mercy, love, and compassion—and He's still speaking and showing up in unexpected ways—even in hard things like a cruel Roman cross.

So if something in Scripture—or in life—makes you pause… or flinch… don't walk away. Don't define God by what you don't yet understand. Trust what you can't yet see.

Remember who He says He is—compassionate, merciful, slow to anger and abounding in love.

And keep seeking Him.

God's Enough

If you find honey, eat just enough—too much of it, and you will vomit.
—Proverbs 25:16, NIV

I have a problem.

Actually, I have several: my wife's gluten-free chocolate chip cookies, all-you-can-eat buffets, and chips and dip—especially chips and dip. I love them… and then I hate myself about an hour later. I eat past the point of fullness and end up writhing in discomfort, can't sleep, and feel awful.

And here's the thing—my wife sees it coming. With love in her eyes and a hand on my arm, she'll say, "You better stop." Or, "That's enough." She's not trying to shame me. She's trying to help me. She knows how I'll feel later. And when I actually listen—when I stop while I'm still feeling good—it's a gift. I feel fine. I sleep well. No regrets. But I don't always listen. I ignore her wisdom and keep eating… and it's not pretty.

Eugene Peterson wrote a great book called, *A Long Obedience in the Same Direction*. It's about the steady, faithful path of following Jesus over time. That's how we want to live. But too often, we find ourselves drifting toward its opposite—a long "disobedience" in the same direction.

This path rarely looks like rebellion. More often, it looks like indulgence. It starts with something good—harmless, even deserved.

But then we keep going. We reach past "enough," blow by wisdom, ignore the quiet whisper of God's Spirit—and eventually, we're sick.

Derek Kidner put words to this deception: *"Beyond **God's enough** lies ecstasy—not nausea."*

You might want to read that again. *It's a lie.* It's the same one the serpent whispered in the garden. The same distortion that pulled King Solomon off course. That "more" will finally satisfy. That God is holding out on you.

But Jesus didn't fall for it.

In the wilderness, when the enemy tempted Him with bread, power, and glory, Jesus said, *"Man shall not live by bread alone, but by every word that comes from the mouth of God."* He trusted the Father. He lived within *God's enough.*

It's a theme that runs throughout Scripture: When God gave manna in the wilderness, it was enough for the day—never for the week. No stockpiles. No hoarding. Just trust. Jesus taught us to pray, "Give us this day our daily bread"—not a warehouse full. Even Paul, tormented by a thorn, heard these words from Jesus: "My grace is sufficient for you." It's enough.

Disobedience doesn't always show up in defiance. Sometimes it looks like just one more bite, one more scroll, one more purchase—one more step away from trust. It starts sweet, but ends with a sour stomach.

Is there something in your life right now that you're chasing past "enough"? Something that started as a gift… but is quietly becoming a god? A long *disobedience* that's subtly pulling you in the wrong direction?

Maybe it's time to listen to the Voice that says, "You've had enough." It's not because God is stingy. Not because He's some kind of killjoy. But because He loves you. Because He sees what's coming and He wants better for you.

The world preaches scarcity, but Jesus offers sufficiency. In Him, we avoid regret and find rest.

He is *God's Enough.*

BECOMING

Becoming Godly

The godly will flourish like palm trees and grow strong like the cedars of Lebanon. For they are transplanted to the Lord's own house. They flourish in the courts of our God. Even in old age they will still produce fruit; they will remain vital and green. They will declare, "The Lord is just! He is my rock! There is no evil in him!"
—Psalm 92:12–15, NLT

Can you name any strong, flourishing, fruit-bearing trees? I can. And no, I don't mean apples, pears, peaches, plums, or apricots. My list includes Bud, Margaret, Ernie, John, Virginia, Jerry, Marlene, Lonnie, and Chris. They're not famous or flashy, but they've stood tall through the seasons of life. Every good gift comes from God, and these "trees" (people) are a gift to me. They embody what the psalmist describes as "godly."

When I think of them, I don't think of perfection—I think of perseverance. They've walked with God through losses and disappointments, through joys and celebrations. Their roots go deep. They read and obey Scripture. They worship wholeheartedly. And as Psalm 92 says, even in old age they are "vital and green." Their lives quietly echo: *"The Lord is just! He is my rock! There is no evil in Him!"*

And the fruit they bear is beautiful—God-glorifying. You can see it in their gentle spirit, a purity that points to Christ, in hope that refuses to quit, and joy that brightens even the darkest day. Their lives are living testimony that when roots go deep in God, the fruit will always draw eyes upward to Him.

Jesus said, *"I am the vine; you are the branches. Those who remain in me, and I in them, will produce much fruit"* (John 15:5, NLT). That's the secret. The godly aren't simply determined people with good habits—they're abiding people with a living connection to Jesus. Their strength and fruitfulness flow from Him.

Notice what the psalm doesn't say. It doesn't say the godly will sit back, coast into retirement, or become consumed by nostalgia, criticism, or cynicism. It says they will still produce fruit. They keep serving, giving, praying, mentoring, and loving. Their eyes aren't fixed on what they've lost or what they're entitled to—they're fixed on Jesus.

Maybe you don't see yourself in the "old age" category yet and think you're off the hook. But the truth is, we're all aging. Each tick of the clock shapes who we are becoming. None of us drifts into godliness. Day by day, choice by choice, we either sink our roots deeper into Christ or we wither in the shallow soil of self.

We're all becoming something. The question is—are you and I becoming godly? Do you want your name on the list of strong, flourishing, fruit-bearing trees? I do.

The only way is to look to Jesus. Stay rooted in Him. Let His life and love flow through you. And the tree of your life will bear fruit that lasts.

Who Are You?

The evil spirit replied, "I know Jesus, and I know Paul, but who are you?"
—Acts 19:15, NLT

I've taken my fair share of "selfies," some with important and popular people, some in exotic places, and scores with friends and family. Honestly, I do it to make memories, but... at times, there is a little part of me that wants to be "known" as one who visits cool places and hangs out with the in-crowd. *Ouch—the blessing and bane of social media... and my pride.*

In Acts 19:13-16, there is a group of Jews called the Seven sons of Sceva who were trying to make a name for themselves (be "known") by going around and casting out evil spirits. They were amassing huge crowds and getting lots of attention by name-dropping... *"in the name of Jesus, whom Paul preaches."*

And it worked—up to a point.

The Sons of Sceva looked good doing and saying what the people wanted. They were casting out evil spirits and garnering lots of "likes" and "followers." But in the end, they were humiliated when one evil spirit they encountered called them out as posers—attacked them, beat them up and exposed them as frauds saying, *"I know Jesus, and I know Paul, but who are you?"*

The evil spirit knew Jesus was the Son of God, the Creator of the universe, the King of Kings, the Lord of Lords, and the Lamb of God who takes away the sin of the world . . . and he trembled (James 2:19). And surprisingly, the evil spirit knew Paul too. But why? It's because Paul's claim to fame was this: *"I have been crucified with Christ and I no longer live, but Christ lives in me. The life I now live in the body, I live by faith in the Son of God, who loved me and gave himself for me"* (Galatians 2:20, NIV).

Paul took the words of Jesus seriously when He said, *"If any of you wants to be "known" as my follower, you must give up your own way, take up your cross daily, and follow me."* (Luke 9:23)

Paul was doing the work of the ministry in Ephesus, but Paul was not the one doing the miracles. It was Jesus who was breaking the strongholds, healing the sick, casting out evil spirits and releasing the captives—and He was doing it through Paul.

Paul knew that all the power and glory belonged to God, and he knew that the only way to really be "known" was not to be seen in scores of "selfies" in this world, but rather be found in a "die-to-selfie" with Jesus.

May we all be "known" in this way.

The Only Real Thing

I have always been a big fan of Pooh, that "silly old bear."

A.A. Milne, the creator of Winnie-the-Pooh, wrote the beloved stories of the Hundred Acre Wood for and about his son, Christopher Robin. In the early 1900s, Pooh and his adventures captured hearts and imaginations, offering comfort and hope to a world reeling in the wake of World War I.

Sometimes, life clouds our view of what truly matters. The world—and even our own reflections in the mirror—distract and overwhelm us with news, conflict, endless controversies, and the harsh, undeniable passage of time. Stories like Winnie-the-Pooh help us rise above the noise, lift our imaginations and remind us of things that are real—like friendship, hope, love, and Truth.

In 1996, the London Times reported that Christopher Milne (the real Christopher Robin) had died at the age of 75. In response, the poet Czeslaw Milosz wrote an anecdote in the voice of Winnie-the-Pooh, reflecting on youth, aging, time and eternity.

> ***Christopher Robin***
>
> *I must think suddenly of matters too difficult for a bear of little brain. I have never asked myself what lies beyond the place where we live, I and Rabbit, Piglet and Eeyore, with our friend Christopher Robin. That is, we continued to live here, and nothing changed, and I just ate my little something.*

Only Christopher Robin left for a moment.

Owl says that immediately beyond our garden Time begins, and that it is an awfully deep well. If you fall in it, you go down and down, very quickly, and no one knows what happens to you next. I was a bit worried about Christopher Robin falling in, but he came back and then I asked him about the well. "Old bear," he answered. "I was in it and I was falling and I wore trousers down to the ground, I had a grey beard, and then I died. It was probably just a dream, it was quite unreal. The only real thing was you, old bear, and our shared fun. Now I won't go anywhere, even if I'm called in for an afternoon snack."

— Czeslaw Milosz*

I love the exchange that Milosz created between Christopher Robin and the "silly old bear." As a child, I adored the stories of Winnie the Pooh—where toys were fast friends and the backyard was a world of adventure, limited only by my imagination.

Milosz's anecdote resonates deeply with me, giving voice to an unexplored realm in Milne's beautiful story, where we all, like Christopher Robin, live in the midst of childlike hope, growing up, old age, and death.

The anecdote begins with Pooh describing the garden where he and his friends live. It is a place of peace and stability, where all abide happily together. Pooh has no idea what lies beyond the garden, nor does he care. Nothing seems to change—except for the fact that he says, "Only Christopher Robin left for a moment."

Pooh knows that his friend Christopher Robin went somewhere. Wise old Owl says that "somewhere" is beyond the garden, where Time begins, and he describes this unknown place as an "awfully deep well."

Pooh lives outside of Time and has no idea that Christopher Robin's "moment" is the deep well of a lifetime (75 years), where he left the garden and entered the world of adulthood—with all of its adventure, hope, pain, joy, loss, and love.

Currently, I am surprised to find that I am like Christopher Robin was in his "moment." I am beyond the garden of childhood innocence and unchecked imagination, and Time is having its way with me. I, in my long trousers and graying whiskers, am free-falling headlong into the unknown deep.

Yet, as I fall, I realize that I am even more like Pooh, a "bear of little brain." Not because I face things I don't understand or care about, but rather, because I forget to fully embrace and appreciate what I already know. I take for granted the fact that each day—and the moments and people that inhabit them—are precious gifts.

So here I am, in the midst of my "moment." It feels very real to me, yet I'm reminded that it isn't—it's, in fact, quite unreal. At this point, my imagination leads me to the only true thing—The Truth. There is something beyond this vapor of life I live. What began in a garden long ago ended victoriously on a cross, and all my "moments" were redeemed and transformed in the depths of an empty tomb.

The author of the truest of anecdotes is Jesus. In Him alone is the place of genuine love, forgiveness, relationship and "shared fun." In Jesus Christ is found the "only real thing," a place where Time is no more; where there are no more tears, regrets, and goodbyes—just life together, in all of its fullness... forever.

Jesus says, *"I go to prepare a place for you"*—a place where we can say, along with Christopher Robin, "I won't go anywhere, even if I'm called in for an afternoon snack."

*Czeslaw Milosz, "Christopher Robin," in New and Collected Poems: 1931–2001 (New York: Ecco, 2003), 656.

The Tree That Is Me

Years ago, I served as an administrator at an international school in South Korea, and one day, Jackie, the office manager, said this to me: "Mr. Roberts, you are 대나무 정령 (daenamu jeongyeong)—'a bamboo spirit.'"

I asked Jackie and the other Korean staff members what that meant in their culture, and they offered the following insights. Bamboo, they explained, symbolizes righteous living in a disorderly world—a combination of upright integrity and accommodating flexibility, perfectly balancing grace and strength. They described how the bamboo tree is resilient and adaptable: it can't be knocked down or broken in a storm but simply bends with the wind. Its hollow center represents purity of spirit and an openness to the divine—embodying someone who lives with resilience, grace, and quiet strength.

Wow, I was deeply humbled by Jackie's kind words and her comparison of me to a bamboo tree. Yet, as I reflect on the tree that is me, I know I fall short of being a true "bamboo spirit."

But oh, how I long to become a "tree" for the Lord and His glory!

The Bible references trees 257 times—more than any other living thing apart from God and people. Throughout Scripture, God's followers are frequently described as, or compared to trees. Consider these verses:

"Blessed is the one … whose delight is in the law of the Lord, and who meditates on His law day and night. That person is like a tree planted by streams of water, which yields its fruit in season and whose leaf does not wither—whatever they do prospers" (Psalm 1:1-3, NIV).

"The righteous flourish like the palm tree and grow like a cedar in Lebanon. They are planted in the house of the Lord; they flourish in the courts of our God. They still bear fruit in old age; they are ever full of sap and green, to declare that the Lord is upright; He is my rock, and there is no unrighteousness in Him" (Psalm 92:12-15, ESV).

Each of us is called to be like the trees in these verses: rooted in God's Word, resilient in trials, and bearing fruit that blesses others. The tree that is me is a work in progress—ever growing and becoming in Him.

Jesus, You are the vine, and I am Your branch. May the tree that is me—whether a mighty oak of righteousness, a majestic cedar planted in Your courts, or even a humble bamboo swaying in the winds of Your Spirit—exist for Your glory.

Are You Dead or Alive?

The path of life leads upward for the wise; they leave the grave behind.
—Proverbs 15:24, NLT

There are 31 chapters in Proverbs, one for every day of the month, and for over 25 years, I've read a chapter a day. They never get old. The timeless words of wisdom speak, guide, convict, and challenge me to live an abundant life.

And yet—what strikes me is how often Proverbs talks about death.

The death Proverbs alludes to isn't just what follows our last breath—it's a death we live in, fully functioning yet far from truly alive. Throughout its chapters, Proverbs contrasts wisdom and folly—wisdom leads to life, while folly leads to death. Beneath this contrast lies the piercing question:

Are you dead or alive?

This question isn't about our final heartbeat—it's about the choices we make every day. Proverbs 8:36 says, *"All who hate me love death."* The "me" refers to the wisdom of God. To reject wisdom is to walk away from the path of life.

King Solomon, the author of Proverbs, traveled this path. Though gifted with immense wisdom, he allowed folly to take root in his life. In his later years, he grew complacent, disobeying God's commands—most notably by marrying multiple foreign wives, which led both him and Israel into idol worship. His choices unraveled his life—for generations—and set the stage for Israel's division and decline. By turning from wisdom, Solomon led the people into spiritual death.

We don't drift into this living death—we choose it. Not in one dramatic moment, but through small acts of apathy, pride, self-centeredness, compromise, and resistance. Over time, life deteriorates—not because God caused it, but because we've traded His wisdom for death.

But here's the hope: We can truly live!

Ephesians 2:5 says, "*…even when we were dead in our trespasses,* [God] *made us alive together with Christ.*"

Jesus—the very wisdom of God—is the way, the truth, and the path to abundant life. He offers us a resurrected, whole new life—now and forevermore.

So, the question remains: Are you dead or alive? We make a choice every day. Choose Wisdom. Choose Life.

Choose Jesus.

Dabbling or Diving

> *This is my endlessly recurrent temptation: to go down to that Sea (I think St John of the Cross called God a sea), and there neither dive nor swim nor float, but only dabble and splash, careful not to get out of my depth and holding on to the lifeline which connects me with my things temporal.*
>
> — C.S. Lewis

What Lewis confesses here isn't just hesitation—it's a lack of trust. A spiritual tug-of-war. And it's where most of us live. We want God, but we resist losing control. The Sea calls, but we cling to the rope. We feel the pull of the eternal, but the comfort of the familiar keeps us in the shallows.

I can relate.

I still remember swimming lessons and the thick rope that stretched across the pool, dividing the shallow end from the deep. I clung to that rope for dear life. One side was safe—I could stand, splash, and stay in control. But the deep end? It was mystery. Risky, wide, and wild… and it scared me.

We're all tempted to play it safe—to cling to the rope of comfort, to hold tightly to the safety lines of routine, relationships, and a rational version of faith. These lifelines give us a sense of control. But they also keep us tethered to the shore—away from the unknown, away from risk, and away from going too deep with God.

But here's the thing: God didn't send His Son to die so we could merely dabble.

In John 21, after the cross, the resurrection, and Peter's denial, we find the disciples in a boat—back to what's familiar. They return to fishing—something they can control, something that doesn't require faith. But their nets are empty—and so are their hearts. Peter is stuck in the shallows of his guilt, shame, and failure—clinging to the strands of a former life.

Then, from the shore, a voice calls: *"Friends, haven't you any fish?"* They don't recognize Him at first. But when the miraculous catch happens, John whispers, *"It's the Lord."*

Peter doesn't hesitate. He throws on his outer garment and jumps. He's not testing the waters. He's all in—plunging into the grace, restoration, and life Jesus offers. Peter went from dabbling to diving. And so must we.

Jesus said, *"I came so they can have real and eternal life, more and better life than they ever dreamed of"* (John 10:10, MSG).

Jesus didn't come and die so we could splash around in the shallows, clinging to the lifeline of what's familiar. He calls us into the depths of His love, where control ends and faith begins.

He calls us to surrender—to let go and lose the life we think we need—so He can give us the life we were truly made for.

Jesus is calling. Let go of the rope. Dive in.

Labels

Therefore, if anyone is in Christ, he is a new creation. The old has passed away; behold, the new has come.
—2 Corinthians 5:17, ESV

Have you ever felt labeled? Like someone sized you up, made a snap judgment, and dropped you into a category without giving you a real chance? I have. And I didn't like it.

We all use labels. Sometimes out loud, but often just in our heads. We're always sorting—people, ideas, even ourselves—into boxes we can manage. It's how we make sense of the world.

But labels can limit. And sometimes they carry more weight than they should. Labels like musical, athletic, artistic, business-minded... religious—they shape how we see people. Some come with admiration. Others come with baggage.

We know what it means when someone is musical. They don't just hum a tune—they play, write, perform. Call someone athletic, and you don't mean they jog on weekends. You mean they compete, move with ease, and excel physically. Say someone is artistic, and you picture creativity spilling out in sketches, color, beauty. A business-minded person sees opportunity, thinks strategically, and knows how to make money.

Each label points to a life—a rhythm, a way of being. But religious? That one often comes weighed down with ritual, judgment, rules and performance. Some prefer the word spiritual. It sounds more personal, more expressive. That's why you often hear, "I'm not religious, but I'm spiritual."

I find Eugene Peterson's comment on Christians and religion interesting:

> *"In some ways Christians are the least religious people in town—there is so much that we don't believe! We don't believe in good-luck charms, in horoscopes, in fate. We don't believe the world's promises or the world's curses."*

Christians don't live by formulas. We live by faith. We're not defined by rituals or spiritual vibes—we're defined by Jesus. And He didn't come to make people religious or spiritual—He came to make us new.

We see this in Jesus' encounter with Nicodemus, one of the most spiritual—and perhaps most religious—men of His day (John 3). Nicodemus was curious—maybe even a little mystical. He came in secret at night, asked thoughtful questions, and had a teachable spirit. And he was "religious" squared—a Pharisee, a leader in the synagogue and a revered teacher in Israel. If anyone could've qualified for eternal life based on tradition, education, or moral effort, it was him.

But as Dallas Willard once wrote, *"Grace is not opposed to effort; it's opposed to earning."*

Nicodemus had the résumé, the training, the reputation, but Jesus wasn't impressed. He was after something deeper.

"Very truly I tell you, no one can see the kingdom of God unless they are born again" (John 3:3, NIV).

No accolades. No performance. Not more awakened. Just... "born again." That phrase might sound dramatic—even outdated—but it's at the very heart of the gospel.

Tim Keller put it simply: *"You don't earn being born. You don't contribute to it. It just… happens. It's grace."*

And so it is with salvation. Jesus didn't offer Nicodemus a better version of his spiritual life. He offered him grace—a new life, rooted in Himself.

The Spirit's work in us isn't to make us impressive. It's to make us new. And not just on Sundays, or when we pray, or do something "sacred." Jesus is after all of it—the spreadsheets and the dishes, the wins and the losses, our time and our tears. He wants us to live a life so full of Him that it spills into everything.

That's what it means to be a Christian. Not religious. Not spiritual. But real… alive in Him. Born again—not better behaved. New creations—not upgraded versions of our old selves.

Christian isn't a label, a category, or a checkbox. It's a life that points—clearly, humbly, unmistakably—to Jesus.

I don't like labels. But that's one I'll welcome.

Been With Jesus

When they saw the courage of Peter and John and realized that they were unschooled, ordinary men, they were astonished and took note that these men had been with Jesus.
—Acts 4:13, NIV

I meet every week with a group of educated young men for Bible study—guys who are genuinely trying to follow Jesus. A few weeks ago, while we were reading Acts 4, Dominic leaned back and said, "I don't buy that Peter and John were unschooled. They spent three years walking with Jesus. Isn't that about the length of time it takes to earn a doctorate?"

We chuckled at his comment—but then sat with it. He had a point.

Peter and John didn't attend rabbinical school, and they didn't carry religious credentials. But they followed the Word made flesh. They ate with Him, traveled with Him, listened to Him teach, watched Him weep, heard Him laugh, and saw Him heal. He didn't just shape their theology; He shaped their entire way of being. It wasn't classroom learning—it was daily apprenticeship with Jesus.

And now, filled with His Spirit, the disciples were doing exactly what He did. Just days earlier, Peter had healed a man who couldn't walk. Then he stood before a hostile council and declared that salvation is found in no one else but Jesus. These weren't timid followers anymore. Their courage, clarity, and authority made it obvious—they had been with Him.

I've spent a lot of time in classrooms, both as a teacher and as a student. And here's what I've learned: godly wisdom doesn't come from seat time. It comes from walking with Jesus. He is the source of Truth. In Him, *"are hidden all the treasures of wisdom and knowledge"* (Colossians. 2:3). He doesn't just inform us—He transforms us. Wisdom doesn't grow through textbooks, but through time in His presence.

In Acts 11, we're told that the early believers were first called "Christians" in the city of Antioch. It wasn't a badge of honor—it was a slur. It meant "those belonging to Christ" or "Christ's men." A label of reproach for people who lived and looked a little too much like Him. The world thought they were fools. But they had been with Jesus—and His Spirit now lived in them—and that made all the difference.

Degrees may impress. Positions might matter. But presence—His presence—is what remains.
The world may call you unschooled, ordinary, even foolish. Fine. Let them. But may one name stick—in its truest sense, not reduced to a label or a title.

Christian—not as a badge we wear, but as a life we live. And most of all, may the world take note—that we have... been with Jesus.

God in the Ordinary

Scrolling Through Life

Anyone who listens to the word but does not do what it says is like someone who looks at his face in a mirror and, after looking at himself, goes away and immediately forgets what he looks like.
—James 1:23-24, NIV

Scrolling is no longer just something we do on our phones and computers—it has become a way of life. We live in an age of distraction. Social media, news, entertainment, and endless notifications pull us in a thousand directions, causing us to skim through everything—important moments, key relationships, engagement with God, and ultimately... life itself.

E. Stanley Jones wisely observed, *"What gets your attention, gets you."* And therein lies the danger of a scrolling heart and life. What is getting our time, our thoughts, our attention, and… our worship?

Distraction isn't just a focus problem. It's a worship problem. True worship isn't realized in rituals or religious practices—it's about where we direct our devotion, commitment, and energy. It's about the things that capture our eyes, our minds, and our hearts.

Eugene Peterson once noted that without worship, we live "manipulated and manipulating lives"—at the mercy of every advertisement, every seduction, every siren. We become vulnerable to whatever demands our attention next, reacting to the world's noise instead of resting in God's voice. Distracted, we forget God… and who we are in Him.

James warns us about treating Scripture the same way we treat our news feeds—glancing at it, then moving on unchanged. God's Word is meant to shape us, not just be another post to scroll through. A mirror shows us who we are, but it only helps if we remember and respond to what we see. God's Word is the same. It reveals our identity in Christ—but if we don't pause to let it shape us, we remain unchanged.

Our thoughts shape who we become. If we allow our hearts and minds to be ruled by distractions, we will conform to the chaos around us. But if we fix our minds on Jesus—meditating on His Word instead of scrolling past it—we will be transformed (Rom. 12:2).

When it comes to attention, the question isn't "What are you looking at?"—it's "What are you worshiping?" Stop scrolling through life and fix your eyes on Jesus, the One who is Life. The only One worthy of all our attention.

Sour Milk

You cannot keep your milk sweet and yet let anything into your dairy; one dirty germ can sour an entire milking. — J.H. Jowett

Blessed is the man who walks not in the counsel of the wicked, nor stands in the way of sinners, nor sits in the seat of scoffers…
—Psalm 1:1, ESV

As a kid, I loved helping my grandad milk his 35 cows on his small farm. He used a vacuum system to pump the milk from the udders into stainless steel buckets, and then he vigilantly strained and filtered the milk into tall, heavy milk cans. Once full, we hammered the lids onto the cans and set them in an icy bath, ready for early morning pickup by the milk hauler.

Each week, my grandad received a check from the milk company—his reward for delivering pure milk. But occasionally, a rejection letter arrived instead. Inside was a stained piece of filter—proof that the milk he provided that week had been contaminated. Whether it was a dead fly, barn dirt, or something unseen, the result was the same: the entire day's milking—all 35 cows' worth—was rejected. One impurity ruined it all.

Just as a speck of dirt can spoil an entire milking, a trace of sin can sour our soul. Psalm 1:1 reveals the deadly decline—it starts small—listening to the wrong voices. Worldly counsel may seem good, but it's not always godly, leading us down a path of doubt, selfishness, and sin.

And before long, we're seated with the scoffers—cynical, critical, and dismissive—and that small trace of sin ultimately taints our entire life.

It's been said, "Sow a thought, reap an action; sow an action, reap a habit; sow a habit, reap a character; sow a character, reap a destiny." The slow souring of the soul begins with a single thought, a small compromise, an unchecked influence, and over time, these choices harden into habits that ultimately shape who we become. We don't wake up one morning dirty and distant from God—it happens gradually—one unfiltered moment at a time.

So what happens when impurities show up? The good news is that while soured milk must be discarded, a soiled soul can be restored—through Jesus, His cross, and the power of His precious blood. In 1 John 1:9, we're given this promise: *"If we confess our sins, He is faithful and just to forgive us our sins and to cleanse us from all unrighteousness"* (ESV).

Are you vigilantly filtering your mind and guarding your heart against subtle contamination? Be sure to look to Jesus! The blessed life is not about perfection—it's about being pure and holy in Him.

Old Wet Tennis Shoes

All of you, dress yourselves in humility as you relate to one another, for "God opposes the proud but gives grace to the humble." So humble yourselves under the mighty power of God, and at the right time he will lift you up in honor.
—1 Peter 5:5-6, NLT

According to the Apostle Peter, what we wear matters. And he isn't talking about power suits and skinny jeans; he's talking about pride and humility. The manner in which we conduct ourselves affects our relationships and interactions, both with God and with others.

Pride is a non-conductor, an insulator that inhibits our connection with God and those around us; whereas humility, as exemplified by Jesus, serves as the conduit in our lives through which God powerfully impacts the world with His love.

As a kid growing up on my Grandad's farm, I learned a valuable lesson about electricity and conductivity that I believe applies to Peter's admonition to "dress yourselves in humility."

At the time, I was wearing a pair of old wet tennis shoes.

In the midst of a busy day of feeding and milking cows, irrigating fields, and maintaining farm equipment, my grandad and I spent some time after lunch mending fence. The tools and materials we needed for the job were in the back of the old farm truck. My grandad asked me to back the rig up to an area of fence that needed some work. Eagerly I complied, but ended up getting the truck a bit too close to the fence—and it was an electric fence.

When my grandad let down the pickup's tailgate it was lying on top of the electric fence wire. My grandad, clad in rubber irrigation boots was unperturbed. He placed one hand on the bed of the pickup and, with a mischievous grin, beckoned me over, extending his weathered hand.

"Grab hold," he said, his eyes twinkling. Obliging and clueless, I squished over to him in my old wet tennis shoes. I reached out, took his hand, and completed the circuit. A jolt of electricity shocked us both!

Grandad's laughter filled the air. Despite the tingling sensation coursing through my veins, I couldn't help but join in. It was a moment of delightful levity, a lesson learned about conductivity, and a metaphor for life.

Pride is a non-conductor. Just as the rubber tires and boots shielded the pickup and my grandad from the electric charge, so too does pride insulate us from the flow of empathy, compassion, and connection with others. Pride stems from thinking too highly of ourselves, and our achievements and circumstances. Pride quenches the Spirit—extinguishing the spark, power, and life of God in our lives. It creates a barrier between us and God and the world around us.

Humility, on the other hand, connects us to God and others, and it is the pathway through which God's power, grace, goodness, and blessing are realized in our lives. Jesus is our model—the Son of God, the King of Kings, and the Lord of Lords, "… *made himself nothing by taking the very nature of a servant, being made in human likeness. And being found in appearance as a man, he humbled himself by becoming obedient to death—even death on a cross!"* (Philippians 2:7-8, NIV)

God extends His hand to us—and to the world around us—through humility. So, as you go about your day, remember Peter's words and "dress yourselves in humility." Put on your old wet tennis shoes and step into the world.

You might find the outcome to be delightfully shocking.

Free Life Jacket

Those who miss me injure themselves. All who hate me love death.
— Proverbs 8:36 NLT

I was at a lake on a hot summer day and noticed a small wooden kiosk by the dock with a sign that read: "Free Life Jackets—Take One." It wasn't fancy—just a rack of sun-bleached orange vests with loose, dangling straps swaying in the breeze. Anybody could take one. No questions asked.

Out on the water, kids splashed and laughed, and swimmers drifted far from shore—few, if any, wearing a life jacket. And I thought… most of us don't give that kiosk a second look.

Life jackets are bulky, uncomfortable, and too hot. They get in the way. And honestly—they just aren't cool. We think, "I'm a strong swimmer—nothing's going to happen to me," until it does… and then it's too late.

The Wisdom of God is a lot like that kiosk—always there, always available, offering help, protection, peace of mind… and life. But most of us walk right past.

Proverbs 8 puts it like this: *"Listen as Wisdom calls out; hear as understanding raises her voice! On the hilltop along the road, she takes her stand at the crossroads. By the gates at the entrance to the town, on the road leading in, she cries aloud… But those who miss me injure themselves. All who hate me love death"* (Proverbs 8:1–4, 36 NLT).

These days, the waters of life are rough—choppy, unpredictable, and dangerous. And every morning, as we step into the maelstrom, there stands the Wisdom of God kiosk—calling out, ready to help and ready to save. Those who miss it risk injury. Those who reject it invite death.

Jesus Christ is that Wisdom kiosk—and the free life jacket. Scripture says, "[He] *is the power of God and the wisdom of God"* (1 Corinthians 1:24, NLT). He knows your heart—your wants, needs, hopes, disappointments, challenges, losses, victories, fears, and failures—and He sees you struggling to stay afloat in troubled waters. And He offers help.

"I love you," Jesus says. "I want to save you. Come to Me, put Me on, and I will give you life."

You can ignore it. You can shrug it off. You can keep swimming on your own.

Or… you can grab the life jacket—and live.

Momma Bear

Better to meet a bear robbed of her cubs than a fool bent on folly.
—Proverbs 17:12, NIV

Years ago, my family was enjoying a sunny day at the water park, and the four of us were swimming in the lazy river. It wasn't too deep—you could walk as easily as float—and my girls, ages eight and six, were having a blast, putting their swimming lessons to good use. People were laughing, playing, splashing around. Others lounged on tubes, and everyone seemed to be having a good time.

All was peaceful… until it wasn't.

My youngest daughter was swimming along when suddenly she slipped under the inner tube of a high school girl who was more interested in tanning and the boy nearby, than in what was happening around her. She didn't notice my daughter was caught underneath her tube.

My wife saw it first. Then I saw something that stunned me. My kind, gentle, soft-spoken wife—small in stature but mighty in that moment—grabbed the tube, flipped the girl into the water, and pulled our daughter up sputtering but safe. She quickly apologized, explained what had happened, and all was fine.

Right then, I felt the full weight of the phrase—*don't mess with a momma bear.*

A mother protecting her child is a force to be reckoned with. But Scripture says there's something even more dangerous: *"…a fool bent on folly."* That's saying something, because a raging bear (and trust me, a protective mom) can be terrifying. But a fool who won't quit is worse. The wreckage never stops—dragging everything down.

When Proverbs talks about a "fool bent on folly," it isn't just picturing one obnoxious person—it's describing a force that's reckless, relentless, and harmful. And in our world, that kind of folly is everywhere. You see it in the endless scroll of social media that never stops to listen. You feel it in the constant churn of news that stirs outrage but never brings peace. You notice it in the distractions we run to that promise escape but leave us anxious and empty.

The danger of folly is this: it won't be corrected, it won't quit, and it won't lead you anywhere good. It subtly pulls you under and leaves you gasping for air. The girl that day in the lazy river just got wet. But folly will drown you. We must stay alert and avoid the deadly drift.

Paul put it this way: *"Be very careful, then, how you live—not as unwise but as wise, making the most of every opportunity, because the days are evil"* (Ephesians 5:15–16, NIV).

Avoid the fool—be wise about what you let shape you. Step away from danger and out of the current of folly. Quiet the noise. Refuse the outrage. Guard against distraction. And fix your eyes on Jesus, for He is wisdom and truth.

He alone will keep you afloat.

Commas Matter

The Spirit of the Lord God is upon me … [to] *proclaim the year of the Lord's favor …*
—Isaiah 61:1–2, ESV

Have you heard the joke about the panda with punctuation problems?

He walks into a café, eats a sandwich, pulls out a gun, fires two shots, and heads for the door. When the staff demands an explanation, he points to a wildlife guide that says:

"Panda: eats, shoots and leaves."

A single comma turns a peaceful lunch into a crime scene. Commas matter.

They may be small, but they shape meaning. A well-placed comma isn't the end of a sentence—it's a pause. A breath. A moment that slows the pace and lets something meaningful settle in.

Pauses like that can bring clarity. But they can also bring discomfort.

Waiting is the name we give to that kind of pause—leaving things uncertain, unfinished, unresolved. Whether you're stuck in traffic, waiting for food to arrive, or listening to the eighth menu option on a customer service call, time moves in slow motion. The minutes drag on, and it seems like nothing is happening. But then, suddenly—the light changes, the food arrives, someone picks up the line—the wait ends, and everything falls into place.

Waiting on God can feel a lot like that.

Suffering lingers. Injustice roars. Prayers echo back in silence. And we start to wonder: Where are You God? Why don't You act?

But Scripture tells us—He is working. Even in the pause.

When Jesus stood in the synagogue in Luke 4 and read from Isaiah 61, He declared His mission: good news for the poor, release for the captives, healing for the broken, and "the year of the Lord's favor." Then… He stopped. Closed the scroll, and sat down.

But the passage He was reading doesn't end there. The next phrase says: "…and the day of vengeance of our God." Jesus left that part out—on purpose. Theologians call that pause "the longest comma in history." It's the gap between His first coming in grace and His second coming in judgment.

And here's the thing—we are living in that comma.

We live in a moment where injustice still reigns, wrongs persist, and God seems quiet. But this isn't divine neglect—it's divine mercy.

As 2 Peter 3:9 reminds us: *"The Lord is not slow in keeping his promise, as some understand slowness. Instead he is patient with you, not wanting anyone to perish, but everyone to come to repentance"* (NIV).

The longest comma in history isn't an inconvenience—it's a gift. A holy pause. In the Lord, when it feels like nothing is happening, something is happening. He's always working. And sometimes, His work takes time.

"Since the world began, no ear has heard and no eye has seen a God like you, who works for those who wait for him!" (Isaiah 64:4, NLT)

One day, what feels unfinished will be complete. What's broken will be made whole. Every injustice will be answered. Every tear wiped away. And Jesus will return.

So we wait—with hope and trust. Jesus is the Author who knows how to punctuate our lives. His pause is mercy. His timing is grace.

Commas matter.

Open the Tent Fly

Even the smallest light can dispel the greatest darkness. —J.R.R. Tolkien

The people who walk in darkness will see a great light. For those who live in a land of deep darkness, a light will shine.
—Isaiah 9:2, NLT

When I was in my twenties I went on a three-day raft trip with my Dad and a couple of other guys. We were on the Smith River, deep in the remote wilderness of Montana. The experience was amazing. On the first night of the trip, Dad and I set up our pup tent, laid out our sleeping bags and quickly fell asleep. We were exhausted from a full day of rowing, exploring and fun.

I tend to be a wild sleeper—prone to talking in my sleep, half-awake/half-asleep moments, and occasional sleepwalking. I awoke in our pup tent in the dead of night, enveloped in complete blackness. We were in the wilderness, with no streetlights or artificial light—just mountains and darkness looming all around—and in my half-asleep state, I panicked.

I couldn't see a thing, and I was scared. My dad tried to console me, gently saying, "It's okay bud, I'm here with you. We're just sleeping in a tent on our raft trip." But in my half-asleep state, I couldn't be calmed. Finally, my dad unzipped the tent fly and told me to look up. The stars were breathtaking—their light pierced the darkness and dispelled my fear. I came to my senses and peacefully went back to sleep.

Even kind words in the darkness couldn't bring me peace. It took the light to dispel my fear. Fear and darkness are intertwined. Just as light dispels darkness, it also dispels fear. The moment I saw the light, my fear faded.

In John 8:12, Jesus says, *"I am the light of the world. Whoever follows me will never walk in darkness, but will have the light of life"* (NIV).

Are you in the dark? Jesus is the light we need. Just as the stars pierced the darkness that night in the Montana wilderness, so does the light of Jesus pierce through the panic and fear in our lives. His light brings clarity in confusion, comfort in anxiety, and peace where there is worry. Darkness, panic, and fear are no match for the light of His love and presence.

Look to Jesus. Open the tent fly of your heart and let Him light up your life.

Show Up

Jesus said, "No procrastination. No backward looks. You can't put God's kingdom off till tomorrow. Seize the day."
—Luke 9:62, MSG

I have a standing meeting every morning at 5:00 a.m. It's on my calendar, though I don't need a reminder dinging on my phone. The meeting is with Almighty God. The agenda? Always the same:

Jesus must become greater; Ryan must become less. (John 3:30)

That's the focus—my walk with Jesus. Sure, with my feet. But mostly with my heart. Because the inner walk is what empowers and sustains the outer one. God started me on this journey, and He's the one who keeps growing me, one step at a time.

At the center of every meeting is this unshakable truth: God loves me and saved me through the blood of His Son, Jesus. He rose from the dead, and He is my hope, my help, and my life. That's the anchor. That's the reason I show up.

So what do I do in these meetings? I pray. I call out for His strength, His Spirit, His wisdom, His love. I open the Bible—God's voice speaking straight into my heart. His Word washes me clean, lights my path, builds my faith. That's non-negotiable—it's always the centerpiece of the meeting.

I'll sometimes bring in other voices too—an author, a teacher, a devotional old or new. They're the "guests" at the table. But they never replace Scripture; they only point me back to it.

And then I write. Journaling helps me reflect, remember, wrestle, and respond to what God is saying. Reflection, I've found, is where roots go deep. It's where growth takes hold.

I try not to miss. Not because I'm keeping score, but because I know who's waiting. Jesus is always there—faithful, present, ready. And every time I show up, I walk away with more than I came in with: strength, help, hope.

Do you have a standing meeting with Jesus? He wants one with you. It doesn't have to be 5:00 a.m. (He's ready whenever you are). Just pick a time, show up, and He'll be there.

That's really all it takes: draw near, lean in, and make yourself available to Him.

Less Talk, More Work

The ideal teacher: someone who can't talk. —William Stafford

During Christmas Break of my last year of college, I worked in a floor covering warehouse with a friend. As we "worked," we were always cracking jokes, talking, laughing, and... goofing around. Every morning, the carpet and vinyl installers parked their trucks in the alley, walked through the warehouse, and headed to the front office to get their job assignments for the day. Most of them greeted us with a friendly smile and hello.

Except for one crusty old installer.

Every day he would grumble the same words as he passed: "Less talk, more work."

That's all he ever said.

He wasn't our boss, and my coworker and I would roll our eyes and laugh it off—but it always stuck with me. How did he know we were talking more than working? Yipes. Did he know Proverbs 10:19: *"When words are many, sin is not absent"* (NIV)?

There sure is a lot of talk these days.

Radio. TV. Internet. YouTube. Podcasts. Social media.

Talk, talk, talk.

Everyone is quick to "speak their truth," tell others how to think, and pass judgment. Criticism abounds. Opinions are shared loudly and often. It's the way of the world, but it's not the way of the Kingdom of God.

In AD 53, the church in Corinth was falling for the same thing—believing that constant critique and spiritual one-upmanship were marks of maturity. But Paul reminded them:

"The Kingdom of God is not just a lot of talk; it is living by God's power" (1 Corinthians 4:20, NLT).

Or as the crusty old installer might have said: "The Kingdom of God is less talk, more work."

When Paul spoke of "living by God's power," he was pointing to Jesus, the ultimate picture of "less talk, more work." John 1:14 says, *"The Word became flesh and made his dwelling among us"* (NIV).

God went to "work" when His Word left Heaven and took on flesh. Jesus didn't just tell us how to live—He lived it. He was kind, merciful, humble, patient, gentle, compassionate, forgiving, faithful, meek, obedient, just, peaceful, and loving. He fed the poor, healed the sick, forgave sinners, turned the other cheek, went the second mile, and took the very nature of a servant.

And then He went to the cross.

"God demonstrates his own love for us in this: While we were still sinners, Christ died for us" (Romans 5:8, NIV). God didn't just say He loved us—He showed us through the "work" of the cross.

No wonder Paul wrote, "The Kingdom of God is not just a lot of talk; it is living by God's power."

So here's the question: Are we talking more than working?

"Less talk, more work."

Maybe the old installer wasn't so crusty after all.

Iron!

Into your hands I commit my spirit; deliver me, Lord, my faithful God.
—Psalm 31:5, NIV

When I was a kid, silver dollars were a big deal. They were large, shiny coins that were cool to look at—and they were money! I always wanted one and my eighty-year-old great-granddad knew it, so at family gatherings he would teasingly play a game with me. He would show me a brand-new silver dollar, then grip the coin in his fist and say, "You can have it if you can get it out of my hand." Easy-peasy, all I had to do was open up his hand and the silver dollar was mine.

I'd go to work—tugging, prying, pounding, twisting, even trying to peel his fingers back one by one. But it was no use. His grip was like iron! I'd sweat and strain while he just sat there smiling, in complete control. I could not get that coin out of his gnarled fist. His strength was amazing.

At last he'd ask, "Ya give?"
I'd nod, exhausted, and then—just like that—he'd open his hand and toss me the silver dollar. It was mine!

"Into your hands I commit my spirit."

King David prayed those words when he was desperate. A thousand years later, Jesus breathed them out with His final breath on the cross—where He died so we might live. We are His treasure, His "silver dollar." And when Jesus placed His spirit into the mighty hands of God, He took us with Him—holding us fast in His nail-pierced hands.

Nothing in all creation is stronger than the love of Jesus. His grip on you is unbreakable. He delights in you, holds you tight, and says, "You are Mine."

So put your life in His hands. You will never regret it—and He will never let you go.

The Gift of Grace and Gratitude

I'm Thankful

Make thankfulness your sacrifice to God.
—Psalm 50:14, NLT

The other day at work, I passed a colleague in the hall who greeted me with, "How are you?" I replied, "I'm thankful." He stopped, smiled, and asked, "What are you thankful about?"

I thought for a moment and said, "Oh wow—lots of things. I'm thankful for the gift of today, my health, this job, my family, my students, God's love in my life… and I'm thankful for you and the chance to work with you."

He paused thoughtfully and said, "Hmmm… there is a lot to be thankful for." Then we both went about our day.

When I responded with, "I'm thankful," I meant it. I wasn't trying to be clever or different—I was simply being real. For a long time, my default answer to "How are you?" was "good," but eventually I realized I couldn't honestly say "good" every time. Life isn't always good. We all have bad days (and sometimes bad years). Life brings moments that hurt, disappoint, and even break us.

But here's the truth that steadies me: "good" isn't the defining factor in my life—Jesus is. And because He is good, I can be thankful.

It's been said that the Apostle Paul wrote about giving thanks and being thankful at least forty-six times in his New Testament letters. It's crazy, but the guy who tells us to *"give thanks in all circumstances"* (1 Thessalonians 5:18) and *"give thanks always… and for everything"* (Ephesians 5:20) is the same guy whose story is filled with persecution, imprisonment, physical suffering, opposition, hostility, shipwrecks, peril, betrayal and abandonment.

How can he be thankful, let alone implore us to be thankful?

It's because thankfulness to God isn't a feeling; it's a choice. Asaph, the author of Psalm 50, even equates thankfulness with sacrifice—giving up something valuable for something even more important or worthy. A life of gratitude doesn't come naturally or easily; it requires practice. It's a discipline. Even the simple habit of praying before meals can be a powerful reminder: each time we eat, we pause to remember God's presence and express gratitude for His care.

Ultimately, the thankfulness that Asaph describes, that Paul commands, and that I mentioned to my colleague, is rooted in Jesus. Jesus is God. He is the author of life, the giver of hope, and the source of every good thing. He is the Creator of the universe, the King of Kings, and the Lord of Lords. His very nature is one of compassion, mercy, love, and grace.

Even while we were all dead in our ingratitude, rebellion, and sin, Jesus took on flesh and blood and came to earth to save us. He died upon the cross, paid the price for the forgiveness of our sins, and rose from the grave. He is our help today and our hope for eternity. Jesus is "good," and a friend who is always with us—even when life stinks. In Him is found joy, peace, hope, and abundant life.

So, if you ask me, "How are you?" I am going to say, "thankful," because of Jesus.

In Him, "…there is a lot to be thankful for."

Refreshment

Then times of refreshment will come from the presence of the Lord.
—Acts 3:19, NLT

It's one of my greatest joys to lead a weekly Bible study with a group of sharp, faith-filled young professionals. These guys are in their mid-twenties—walking with God and hungry to grow in their faith. We're working our way through the book of Acts, and recently we came to the moment in chapter 3 when Peter and John encountered a man who had been crippled from birth. He was expecting coins from them—but what he got was healing.

It was a miracle, and a crowd gathered—full of questions.

Peter—never one to miss a moment—pointed straight to Jesus and said, "You handed Him over. You denied the Holy and Righteous One. You killed the Author of life, but God raised Him from the dead."

The people hadn't understood who Jesus really was—not then, but now they did. And Peter extended the invitation: *"Now repent of your sins and turn to God, so that your sins may be wiped away. Then times of refreshment will come from the presence of the Lord"* (Acts 3:19, NLT).

That last line caught us.

One of the guys said, "I've heard of peace and joy. But I've never heard of… refreshment." Another nodded. "Yeah. What exactly is that?"

We all sat with it for a moment—curious, amazed, longing. We let it sink in. We knew that feeling—or maybe more honestly, we knew our need for it. Not just peace or joy, but something deeper—something we hadn't had words for until now.

Refreshment. Not a break. Not a pause. But a real, soul-deep restoring. Like water on dry ground. Like catching your breath after a hard workout.

That Bible study conversation stayed with me. A few days later, still thinking about what refreshment really means, I bumped into this line in Jeremiah 45:5, *"I will give you your life as a reward wherever you go"* (NLT).

That's a promise spoken to the scribe Baruch, at a time of chaos, in a culture crumbling at the edges. God wasn't promising ease. He was promising something better—Life. Real life. Whole life. A life that doesn't rise and fall with the headlines, the markets, or the mood of the day.

And it hit me—that is refreshment. Not escape from trouble. Not the absence of struggle. But the presence of God in it all. When we surrender to Him—truly let go of control, fear, and our sin—we don't just survive. We breathe again. We live—fully, freely… refreshed.

Hundreds of years after Jeremiah and Baruch, Jesus said, *"I have come that they may have life, and have it to the full"* (John 10:10, NIV).

Let that sink in today.

Peter made it clear to the crowd then, and to you and me now: Jesus, the One who was crucified and raised—the One who heals, forgives, and restores—is still inviting us to come, to repent, and to receive… refreshment.

Worth It

Is anything worth more than your soul?
—Matthew 16:26, NLT

Have you ever wandered through a yard sale and felt that quiet tension between buyer and seller? The seller lays out their timeworn pieces, each priced high, carrying not just a dollar amount, but history and an emotional attachment. Every item has a story—a reminder of its usefulness and the memory of its original cost.

The buyer doesn't see or appreciate any of that. They're only looking for a deal. When they make a lowball offer, it stings. The seller rejects it outright. And the buyer just shrugs, turns away, and says, "It's not worth it."

"Worth it."

It's more than just a phrase—it's the filter we use to measure almost everything in life. What's worth your time, your money, your energy? What's worth...you?

The worth of anything is measured by what someone is willing to give in exchange for it. Did you know that in God's economy, your soul—your very self—is of inestimable worth? So valuable, in fact, that He gave the life of His one and only Son in exchange for you.

But here's the twist: in the marketplace of life, we are the ones who decide what our soul is worth. We choose what we're willing to trade it for—approval, status, pleasure, influence, security, success, control. The world doesn't value people the way God does. It has its own ideas of worth, constantly pressuring us to sell out for the next shiny thing. Society measures value by usefulness, beauty, and influence—but God looks at the heart.

Scripture warns us not to fall for the Esau syndrome—trading away God's lifelong gift in order to satisfy a short-term appetite (Hebrews 12:16–17, MSG). Esau sold his birthright for a bowl of stew. He walked away with a full stomach—but an empty soul.

Your soul is not a discount item. It's not something to trade for fleeting pleasures or worldly applause. You are the apple of God's eye—His beloved—fearfully and wonderfully made. And while the enemy is happy for you to sell your soul—whether for millions or for a moment—God calls you to hold out for the higher price, the one that reflects your true, immeasurable worth.

King David once asked, *"What are mere mortals that you should think about them?"* (Psalm 8:4, NLT). Centuries later, the Apostle Paul gave the answer: *"But God showed his great love for us by sending Christ to die for us while we were still sinners"* (Romans 5:8, NLT).

That's your value.

So be vigilant. Guard your eyes, your ears, your heart, and your mind. Every moment of every day, you're deciding what your soul is worth. Don't let the world write that price tag—because Jesus already did.

And He says, "You're worth it."

Beauty

The fairest thing… is Christ Himself. — Richard Sibbes

Have you ever been left speechless?

I can't even begin to describe that golden sunset at the Oregon Coast, the kaleidoscope of life and color housed in the coral reef of Thailand, or the smiles on the faces of orphans in India as they laugh and play with a brand-new soccer ball. There are no words.

Think of the hush of a mountain lake at sunrise in the Sawtooths, where the only sound is the splash of a fish rising. Or the first snowfall of winter—white and silent. Or music that stirs something deep within you, as if heaven itself brushed against your soul. There are no words.

But all that pales in comparison to the profound beauty of my two daughters, and memories of them as precious newborn babies, cute and comical toddlers, smiling schoolchildren, laughing teenagers, adventurous and determined college students, and committed followers of God. I can't get over their hugs, and their love for each other, for their mother, and for me.

There are no words.

And yet, all that beauty—even the most beautiful thing you and I can think of—is but a shadow of the radiant grandeur of the heart of God. Consider this: "*For God so loved the world, that he gave his only Son, that whoever believes in him should not perish but have eternal life*" (John 3:16, ESV).

When we were utterly helpless, Christ came at just the right time … and God showed his great love by sending him while we were still sinners (Romans 5:6–8, NLT).

That's a beauty we didn't earn, don't deserve, and can never lose—a gift that calls for gratitude.

Jesus said, *"I am the bread of life. Whoever comes to me will never be hungry again. … I will never reject them"* (John 6:35, 37 NLT).

Jesus will wipe every tear from their eyes, and there will be no more death or sorrow or crying or pain. … He says, "Look, I am making everything new!" (Revelation 21:4–5, NLT).

It's splendor timeless and eternal—that death cannot erase and eternity will only deepen.

O the beauty.
There are no words, except one…

Jesus.

Love Is All That Matters

Though he was God, [Jesus] *did not think of equality with God as something to cling to. Instead, he gave up his divine privileges; he took the humble position of a slave and was born as a human being. When he appeared in human form, he humbled himself in obedience to God and died a criminal's death on a cross.*
—Philippians 2:6–8, NLT

I have two daughters, now grown. But when they were born, my world changed forever. It was the beginning of the greatest years of my life.

When they were little, I wore a lot of hats at work—pastor, teacher, professor, school administrator. People called me by all sorts of titles: leader, supervisor, boss. And those titles mattered. They opened doors, carried responsibility, and helped me provide for my family.

But here's the thing: when I walked through the front door of our home, none of that mattered. Not one bit. To my girls, I wasn't "Pastor Ryan" or "Professor Roberts," or "The Principal." I was just Daddy. The one who wrestled on the living room floor, read bedtime stories, and kissed scraped knees. They didn't need my credentials. They just needed me—present, loving, ... theirs.

And that, I think, is a glimpse of how Jesus loves us.

Think about it. Jesus is God—eternal, infinite, the Alpha and Omega. His names and titles stretch farther than we can even grasp: Son of God, Prince of Peace, Immanuel, Lord of Lords. He's the Creator of galaxies, the One who sustains the universe by the power of His word.

And yet… He laid it all down.

He didn't cling to His position. He didn't hold onto the recognition He rightfully deserved. Instead, He humbled Himself. He came not as a warrior, but as a baby. Not to be served, but to serve. Not to demand, but to give.

Why? Just one word—love.

When He saw you and me stuck in sin, lost in the dark, unable to save ourselves, He didn't stay distant. He didn't leave us to figure it out. He came close. He stooped low. He chose the cross. Not because we deserved it. Not because He owed us. But because love says, "You're worth it."

Sometimes I wonder what the angels must have thought—watching the King of Glory wash dirty feet… be mocked by crowds He created… hang, bleeding, on a wooden beam He Himself designed. I imagine Heaven understood what we so easily forget—the truest thing about Jesus isn't His power. It's His heart. And His heart is love.

That's the name He carried when He came for us.
The title He bore when He died for us.
And it's the banner He still holds over us.

Love… is all that matters.

That Simple

The other day I bumped into a friend I hadn't seen in ages. Totally unexpected. We only had about five minutes to catch up.

We traded the usual updates about work and family, and then—almost out of nowhere—the conversation turned to faith.

"My relationship with God has been kind of cold lately," he said, eyes dropping. "I just feel… off."

I felt for him. I've been there. It's a hard place to be. You feel like you've failed somehow, and the way back to God seems complicated—like there's a long list of things you've got to fix before you can even try.

I wanted to give him something, anything, that might help. And what popped into my mind was James 4:8: *"Draw near to God and he will draw near to you"* (ESV).

I shared it with him. He was quiet for a moment, then asked, "Is it really that simple?

And suddenly our five minutes were up.

If we'd had a few more minutes, I would have reminded him of the Father standing on the road, watching for the prodigal's return (Luke 15). I would have told him that God is faithful, even when we're not

(2 Tim. 2:13). And that Jesus never gives up on us—He's still knocking at the door (Rev. 3:20).

As we parted, I promised to pray for him. I encouraged him to read his Bible and call out to the Lord in prayer.

I told him, "Start there—draw near to God, and He'll draw near to you."

Thanks to Jesus, it really *is* that simple.

Enough

Jesus made a whip from some ropes and chased them all out of the Temple.
—John 2:15, NLT

Every year, April 15th rolls around—Tax Day. And every year, I hold my breath, wondering if I did the math right, hoping maybe this time I'll get a return. But somehow, I always end up owing more. I'm never quite sure why. The rules keep changing... or maybe it's just me. Either way, it's always the same: whatever I've done—it's never quite enough.

That feeling—never quite enough—isn't new. God's people knew it well. They experienced it every year during Passover. The Passover celebration was a time to remember—when the blood of a lamb over the door frame of your home meant rescue, deliverance, and salvation. It was a night when judgment passed over. It was a shadow of something greater to come.

For centuries after that first Exodus, people streamed into Jerusalem and gathered in the Temple courts to observe Passover and honor God with a sacrifice. They came from distant towns and surrounding villages, bearing offerings—hoping to pay their dues for mercy and forgiveness.

But there were rules. First, they had to exchange their money at an unfair rate and then buy a lamb, a dove, or two pigeons for an outrageous price. They paid extravagantly for something that was never enough. Year after year. Sacrifice after sacrifice. Blood upon blood. It was a vicious and empty cycle.

And then Jesus came.

He walked into the Temple and saw what God's house had become—a business, a machine, a place where grace was sold at a markup. He saw the injustice, the swindling, the shell of religion that burdened the people but never freed them—and He had seen enough.

With a whip of cords, He overturned tables, sent coins flying, and drove out the merchants who had turned His Father's house into a den of thieves. He didn't just flip tables that day—He flipped the whole system—the way humanity understood access to God. The doves took flight, the cattle fled, the sheep scattered... and grace came running.

When the dust settled, there were no sacrifices left in the building.

None, except One.

The Lamb of God who takes away the sin of the world stood alone in the Temple courts, steady and unshaken—like a tree on a hill.

It was a glimpse of what was coming. Because days later, on a hill called Calvary, Jesus paid the ultimate, extravagant price—once and for all—for the religious, the swindlers, the broken, the lost... and for you and me.

On the cross, He shed His blood and spoke words that shattered every system, silenced every sacrifice, and sealed our salvation forever:

"It is finished." No more striving. No more endless atonement. Nothing between us and the love of God.

Jesus… is enough.

The Perfect Picture

You're nothing but a mist, a wisp of fog, catching a brief bit of sun before disappearing.
— James 4:14, MSG

As a budding photographer, I've learned that fog is elusive—constantly shifting, moving, and vanishing. You have to act fast to capture the shot because with fog, it's there one moment, and gone the next. But when the light and mist align, something extraordinary happens—a brief moment of breathtaking beauty—the perfect picture.

I think that's what James had in mind when he spoke about our lives—we are all a mist—brief, beautiful, and then gone. Psalm 39:5 reminds us, *"Everyone is but a breath, even those who seem secure"* (NIV). Rich or poor, powerful or weak, young or old, no one outruns time. Left to ourselves, our days slip by—unremarkable. But in the Lord, our lives can take on lasting beauty.

Jesus is, *"the light of the world"* (John 8:12, NIV). He is the *"bright morning star,"* and when the mist of our lives reflects His light we become more than a passing vapor. We embody a radiance and beauty that transcends time.

Light gives life. A stained-glass window without light is just darkened glass—its beauty unseen, its purpose unfulfilled. But when light floods through it, the colors glow, and its true design is revealed. In the same way, a life without Jesus is like mist in the dark—formless and unseen.

But when His Spirit shines through us—even for a moment—we glisten with beauty.

The light of Jesus takes our ordinary moments and fills them with His glory. A song becomes more than just music, a sermon more than just words, and an act of kindness more than just a good deed. A whispered prayer, a cup of cold water given in His name, a word spoken in love—each one, touched by His light, carries a glory that outlasts us.

We're not perfect, and no matter how hard we try, we cannot create lasting glory for ourselves. But we can reflect the glory of Jesus, the One who lasts forever.

Let His love illuminate the mist that is your life. When you do, you become—in that moment—the perfect picture of His breathtaking beauty.

Christ and the Cross

Unto You

"Now I finally know the real meaning of Christmas."

I'll never forget the Christmas Eve my family and I spent with our friend Jaeyoung in Daejeon, South Korea. It was a cold, snowy night—just the way Christmas Eve is supposed to be—and we walked from our apartment to Jaeyoung's restaurant for dinner.

The restaurant was tiny—only three tables—and packed when we arrived. Some customers were seated and eating, others stood waiting for takeout. Jaeyoung and his wife were well loved in that part of the city, known for two things: their good food and their warm friendship.

We finally got a table, and Jaeyoung and his wife showered us with care and attention—they adored our daughters. The meal was delicious. As the evening wore on, the crowd thinned, and before long we were the only ones left. We had nowhere else to go and wanted to linger with our Korean friends.

Jaeyoung pulled a chair close and sat with us. Our Korean was limited, but his English was good enough for a real conversation. He was quiet for a moment, his eyes slowly scanning the room—the flashing lights in the window, the Santa picture taped to the door, the worn tree standing in the corner. His gaze lingered there before he turned back to me. And then, with a seriousness that caught me off guard, he asked,

"What is the real meaning of Christmas?"

I paused, letting his question sink in.

Is Christmas all about Santa, the Grinch, Rudolph, Frosty, gifts, toys, trees, decorations, and twinkling lights? These are all part of the season as we know it, bringing joy and color, filling it with fun and festivity. But Christmas is more than that—so much more.

I told Jaeyoung about God's deep love for all people—how He created the universe and made us His most treasured possession. God desires a relationship with us as His children. He is love. And in love, He gave us free will—the choice to love Him back. But we chose otherwise. Our sin separated us from the holy God.

The whole story of Scripture is about God's relentless pursuit of us—His call to bring us home. And in the greatest act of love, God sent His Son, Jesus, into the world. Jesus came as God in the flesh to reveal the Father's heart, to die for our sins, and to rise again—offering us forgiveness and the hope of eternal life.

And then, right there in that little restaurant, my mind went to Linus—standing on a quiet, dimly lit stage—answering Charlie Brown's question:

"Isn't there anyone who knows what Christmas is all about?"

I smiled and shared Luke 2:8–12 with Jaeyoung:

> *"And there were in the same country shepherds abiding in the field, keeping watch over their flock by night. And, lo, the angel of the Lord came upon them, and the glory of the Lord shone round about them: and they were sore afraid. And the angel said unto them, Fear not: for, behold, I bring you good tidings of great joy, which shall be to all people. For unto you is born this day in the city of David a Savior, which is Christ the Lord. And this shall be a sign unto you; Ye shall find the babe wrapped in swaddling clothes, lying in a manger"* (KJV).

Then I leaned in and said, "Jaeyoung, the real meaning of Christmas isn't about Santa, gifts, trees, and lights. It isn't even about the three wise men, Mary and Joseph, or a baby lying in a manger.

Listen to what the angel said: *"…unto* ***you*** *is born this day in the city of David a Savior."*

Unto you.

Christmas is about you and me—and God's love for each one of us."

John the disciple says it well: *"This is how God showed his love among us: He sent his one and only Son into the world that we might live through him"* (1 John 4:9, NIV).

That night, in that tiny restaurant, the message broke through. Christmas isn't just about nativity scenes or holiday traditions. It isn't even just about God's miraculous act. Christmas is about us — and the God who loves us.

Jaeyoung sat quietly for a moment, taking it all in. Then his face softened, and a smile slowly spread across it. He placed his hand over his heart and said, almost in a whisper,

"Now I finally know the real meaning of Christmas."

The Tree…It's Already There

He himself bore our sins in his body on the tree…
—1 Peter 2:24, ESV

Before I ever knew Jesus as my Savior, I knew a song about Zacchaeus and a sycamore tree. As a kid, my grandma occasionally took me to church. The children gathered in the damp church basement and I remember flannel graph stories on the felt board, cookies and punch, and songs with motions that we sang at the top of our lungs. One of those songs went like this:

> *Zacchaeus was a wee little man, a wee little man was he.*
> *He climbed up in a sycamore tree for the Lord he wanted to see…*

Back then, it was just a fun song—but now I see it meant so much more.

In Luke 19 we find that Zacchaeus wasn't just a "wee little man." He was a man who was lost. A tax collector who was hated and despised. He was a Jew in bed with Rome, and his sin wasn't hidden—it was public, notorious, and shameful. Yet there he was, climbing up a tree, wanting to see Jesus. He was a man deeply in need of a grace that he didn't even know existed.

The tree itself was ordinary—just a tree along the dusty road. But when Zacchaeus climbed it, something changed. That tree became a holy place—an unexpected avenue where Jesus would stop, look up, and call him by name.

According to theologians, that tree served as "prevenient grace" in Zacchaeus's life. In simple terms, it means "going before." It's the kindness of God that reaches for us before we reach for Him. It's God wooing us unto Himself.

It's that nudge—the tug in your heart to look to Jesus. It's more faithful than a praying grandmother. More beautiful than a song you remember from childhood. It's love—pure and persistent. It's Jesus walking the road you didn't know you'd be on, calling your name before you even thought to look up.

Zacchaeus wanted to see Jesus. But the truth is, Jesus was already looking for him. That sycamore tree was the bridge that brought him face to face with the Savior.

There is another tree that stands in the path of all of us—the tree upon which Christ was crucified. And just like the tree Zacchaeus climbed, the cross goes before us, serving as a bridge to new life. The cross of Christ is where our sins are forgiven. It is the means by which we are saved.

I am Zacchaeus—and so are you. Jesus is always going before us, wooing us unto Himself. He can take anything—an old church basement, a loving grandmother, even a silly song—and use it for good in our lives.

He is already looking, already loving, and already preparing the way for you and for me.

And the tree? … It's already there.

They Really Lived

Sirs, what do I have to do to be saved—to really live?
—Acts 16:30, MSG

One of my favorite movies is *Secondhand Lions*. It tells the story of two eccentric old uncles, Hub and Garth, who spend their latter days sitting on the porch, shooting at trespassing traveling salesmen, and bemoaning days gone by. In their youth, they fought wars, hunted wild animals, and chased treasure and adventure at every turn. They even battled—and eventually befriended—a rich and powerful sheikh in North Africa.

Their story is told by their nephew, Walter, who grew up living with these two uncles. In the final scene, after his uncles have passed, Walter, now an adult, is approached by another man—the grandson of the very sheikh from his uncles' stories—with a question full of wonder: "So, the two men from my grandfather's stories, they really lived?"

Walter nods and replies, "Yeah… they really lived."

It's a simple statement, but it lingers. "They really lived." Not just existed, not just survived…but truly, fully…lived.

What does it mean to really live?

This isn't just an abstract idea—it's a question as old as time. Two thousand years ago, a Philippian jailer, shaken to his core, asked Paul and Silas the very same thing: *"Sirs, what must I do to be saved—to really live?"* (Acts 16:30, MSG).

Our world is obsessed with the idea of an extraordinary life. Social media floods us with highlight reels, fueling the fear that we're missing out on something bigger and better. At first glance, Hub and Garth seem to embody real life. But Scripture tells us otherwise—true life isn't about chasing adventure—it's about trust. A deep, full, soul-satisfying life comes from trusting Jesus, the One who is the way, the truth and the life.

Paul and Silas didn't tell the jailer to do more or try harder. Their answer was simple: *"Put your entire trust in the Master Jesus. Then you'll live as you were meant to live"* (Acts 16:31, MSG).

To really live isn't about a constant search for meaning, always chasing something just out of reach, or writing the wildest, most adventurous story with your life—it's about trusting in the One who wrote life itself. It's about walking with Jesus, knowing Him, and letting His presence fill your days with purpose.

So stop striving for life where it cannot be found. Trust Jesus. Abide in Him.

And really live.

Engagement Ring

When you believed in Christ, he identified you as his own by giving you the Holy Spirit, whom he promised long ago. The Spirit is God's guarantee that he will give us the inheritance he promised and that he has purchased us to be his own people. He did this so we would praise and glorify him.
—Ephesians 1:13–14, NLT

Nearly forty years ago I asked Dina to marry me, and when I did, I gave her an engagement ring. It was a token of my love, a sign of my commitment to her—and to us. That little ring was a tangible symbol of my future intentions.

Buying it wasn't easy. I was still in college, counting pennies to get by. I did odd jobs, saved every bit I could, and finally bought the ring. It cost me $100—a fortune to me at the time—but it was worth every cent. That ring represented more than money. It was an investment in my preferred future: Dina and me, together.

Much to my delight, Dina wore the ring proudly. It was a statement to everyone around her that she was loved and cherished. It pointed to a promise, a future hope, a dream that would one day be fulfilled. That simple band changed the way we saw ourselves and how we interacted with the world around us.

Paul says in Ephesians 1 that the Holy Spirit is God's guarantee to His people—His down payment on the promise of eternal life with Him. The Spirit is, in a way, our engagement ring from Jesus. It is the pledge of God's love, the "already but not yet" promise of His Kingdom in our midst. It clarifies our identity, sets our purpose, and reminds us that we belong to Him. It quietly declares, *"I am His, and He is mine."*

The Spirit's presence in our lives reshapes everything—how we live, love, work, and walk in the world. It calls us to faithfulness, sacrifice, and hope as we await the day when the promise is fully realized.

The ring I bought for Dina cost me $100. The "engagement ring" God gave us cost Him His Son. Receive the gift. Walk in the Spirit. Wear it proudly and joyfully.

Let your life be a living sign that you... belong to Him.

The Light *[A Christmas Reflection]*

The people who sat in darkness have seen a great light. And for those who lived in the land where death casts its shadow, a light has shined.
—Matthew 4:16, NLT

I was only five years old, but I still remember the light.

It was Christmas Eve, 1971. After my dad got off work, our family—my mom, dad, baby sister, and I—all loaded into our family car, a 1969 Volkswagen Bug, and headed for my grandparents' home in Jerome, Idaho to celebrate Christmas with a house full of aunts, uncles, cousins, loving family, and fun. It was snowing and blowing when we left Boise.

What was supposed to be a two-hour journey turned into a long, slow drive into a dark and snowy night. The wind blew, and the snow swirled the entire trip, blanketing everything in white.

We finally turned off the main road onto the quarter-mile long lane that led to my grandparents' farmhouse and were surprised to find that drifting snow had formed a barrier across our path.

My dad, hoping to break through the drifts, accelerated the car—and I was thrilled. I remember the roar of the VW engine, the unsettling sound of snow scraping on the floorboards beneath our feet, and the car slowly coming to a dead stop.

Our headlights were buried under snow, and with the engine running we sat there in total darkness—completely stuck.

Still a long way from the house, all we could do was trek the remaining distance on foot. It wasn't going to be easy for my parents—trudging through the deep snow with a baby, a five-year-old, and all of our belongings.

However, a glimmer of hope appeared in the dark night. Down the lane, a flashlight flickered and slowly moved toward us. It was my granddad on his tractor, making his way through the snow to our rescue.

I was captivated by that light. It was just a flashlight, but it pierced the darkness. As it approached, the outline of the tractor chugging through the snow emerged, and then, finally, I could see the smile on my granddad's face.

He leaped off the tractor, gave us all hugs, hooked a chain to the front of the car, and pulled us home through the swirling snow. Within minutes we were enveloped in the radiant glow of love, family, and a joyous Christmas celebration.

Where do you find yourself this Christmas? Feeling stuck? Trapped? Lost in the darkness? Here's some good news—a glimmer of hope. *"The angel said to them, 'Fear not, for behold, I bring you good news of great joy that will be for all the people. For unto you is born this day in the city of David a Savior, who is Christ the Lord.'"*

There it is, the real meaning of Christmas. A light has dawned and the rescuer has come to bring us home—it is Jesus.

Over fifty years later, I still remember that Christmas Eve—the long trip, the dark night, getting stuck in the snow, my grandfather's smile, and the joyous fun.

But most of all ... I remember the light.

The G.O.A.T.

The Son of God came to destroy the works of the devil.
—1 John 3:8, NLT

In every dorm room debate, group text thread, or sports documentary, the question always comes up: Who's the G.O.A.T.? —the Greatest of All Time.

Is it Jordan or LeBron? Brady or Montana? Serena or Steffi? Messi or Ronaldo? The arguments rage on, stats are compared, highlight reels analyzed. Everyone has their pick. But there's one G.O.A.T. whose greatness surpasses trophies, titles, or talent. His arena wasn't a court or field—it was a cross. His victory wasn't won with a ball or a racket, but with the weight of our sin upon His shoulders.

In Leviticus 16, God gave Moses instructions for the Day of Atonement—a day when Israel's sins were symbolically dealt with through two goats. One was sacrificed. The other, the scapegoat, was brought before the priest, who would lay his hands on its head and confess over it the sins of the people. Then the goat was led far away into the wilderness, carrying all the guilt, shame, and sin of the people out of the camp… never to return.

It's a haunting picture—and a holy one.

Thousands of years later, we see Jesus—the true scapegoat—bearing not just symbolic sins, but the real, soul-staining filth of humanity. Paul writes in 2 Corinthians 5:21, *"God made him who had no sin to be sin for us, so that in him we might become the righteousness of God"* (NIV). Jesus didn't just carry our sins away—He became sin for us.

And He didn't stop there.

He doesn't just remove our guilt—He destroys its power. *"Having disarmed the powers and authorities, he made a public spectacle of them, triumphing over them by the cross"* (Colossians 2:15, NIV).

The Enemy, through sin, had us locked in shame. But Jesus took all that sludge—our guilt, our fear, our unworthiness—and hauled it upon Himself, back to hell where it belongs. The fiery darts of the wicked one hold no power over us because Jesus, our scapegoat, has removed them—as far as the East is from the West.

So, who's the real G.O.A.T.?

Not the one with rings or records, but the One with the scars.
Not the one who entertains crowds, but the One who redeems them.
Jesus is the greatest of all time—not just because of what He did, but because of who He is—the Risen King.

And now, because of Him, we stand forgiven, free… victorious!

The Scarlet Thread

Author's Note: What follows is a creative retelling of Joshua 2. It isn't meant to be a replacement for Scripture, but an imaginative "what if?" woven from the biblical account. The identities of the two spies Joshua sent are unknown, but here I've wondered—could one have been Caleb, and could the other have been Salmon, who later married Rahab and became part of the line of Christ? This piece takes creative liberty while staying rooted in the scarlet thread of redemption we see throughout the Bible. Think of it less as commentary and more as a story that invites reflection.

Tie this scarlet cord in the window through which you let us down…
—Joshua 2:18, ESV

Caleb was tired of waiting. Forty years had passed since he and Joshua had torn their robes in frustration—begging the people to trust God and take the land. But the people listened to the ten spies, and Joshua and Caleb spent the next forty years digging graves for a faithless generation.

But now… it was time to enter the Promised Land. Joshua was in charge, and he turned to Caleb and said, "We need eyes on Jericho."

Caleb nodded. "I have someone."

Salmon was young, but not green. He was the kind of man who listened more than he spoke. He walked with God, moved like a shadow, and carried a quiet discernment that set him apart. He was a rising warrior from the tribe of Judah—and one of Caleb's finest protégés.

When Caleb approached him that morning, Salmon stood, spear in hand, dressed and ready. Caleb smiled, "We've got work to do."

Jericho loomed—massive and imposing, but not invincible. They entered the city under cover of dusk, blending in with a caravan of merchants at the gate. Caleb kept to the shadows while Salmon scouted ahead. They knew they were being watched.

`Then came a whisper— "This way." And they followed. The voice belonged to a woman. Her name was Rahab. She led them up a narrow staircase, into a room of thick curtains, colorful linens, and strong perfume. "I know who you are," she said. "Everyone in Jericho does."

Then came the pounding at the door—loud, urgent. It was the king's men, and she acted quickly. She hid the men under a pile of flax on the roof and spun a tale of travelers who had been there but had already fled the city. Her ruse worked.

That night, under the stars, she spoke quietly to the men: "We've heard about your God—how He dried up the Red Sea. How He gave you victory over Egypt. Everyone here is terrified…but I believe. I believe your God is the true God."

Salmon stared at her. Not with suspicion—but with wonder. She wasn't like anyone he'd met before. Her faith was raw, desperate…real. Caleb watched him watching her. And he knew.

The spies made a promise. Rahab had saved them—and they would save her. Before they slipped into the hills, they turned to her one last time. "Tie this scarlet cord in your window. When we return, it will be the sign."

The scarlet cord was a symbol of mercy—the thread of salvation. Rahab let them down through the window and left the cord tied in place. The spies vanished into the hills, and three days later they stood before Joshua. Salmon reported, "The Lord has surely given us the land."

Caleb didn't speak of Rahab. But later, when Jericho's walls fell, he turned to the young man and said quietly, "Go get her."

Salmon did, and years later, their son would be named Boaz. He'd be a man of kindness. A redeemer. A beautiful strand in the patchwork of redemption. And when the family line was recorded, Boaz was named—and so was his mother, Rahab—once an outsider, now woven into the story of salvation.

Generations later, another child was born in that family line—and the scarlet thread of hope continued. Not through a rope, but as a promise.

In a person—Jesus.

He Said Nothing

He gave him no answer, not even to a single charge…
—Matthew 27:14, ESV

We've all been there—accused unfairly, talked about behind our backs, ambushed in a conversation, criticized, or "set straight" by someone who didn't come with kindness. It wasn't gentle correction—it was an attack. If you're like me, you wanted to defend yourself. And maybe… you did.

These days, outrage is everywhere. From cable news feeds to coffee shop tables to social media threads, people are quick to quarrel—convinced they're right and ready to fight. And if I'm honest—I get it. I've felt the pull: mind racing, gut churning, heart pounding with indignation, forming the perfect response, rehearsing what I'd say.

But then—I remember Jesus.

He stood before Pilate, falsely accused and completely misunderstood, and Matthew tells us, *"He gave him no answer, not even to a single charge"* (Matthew 27:14, ESV). Jesus—the only truly "right" and righteous One—didn't scramble to defend Himself. He didn't try to win the argument.

He said nothing.

That kind of restraint is hard for me. I want to defend my honor—explain, justify, make my case, and prove I'm right. But Proverbs 20:3

redefines my definition of honor: *"It is to one's honor to avoid strife, but every fool is quick to quarrel"* (NLT).

The world applauds quick comebacks and strong opinions, but wisdom sees through the noise. Commentator Derek Kidner put it plainly: "To spring to the defense of one's honor is to do it a disservice." When I rush to protect my pride, I often end up harming the very thing I was trying to preserve. Am I really defending truth—or just defending myself?

There's a sacred dignity in silence. It's not apathy—it's anchored trust. Trust that God sees. That truth holds. That Jesus is the way.

The Lord didn't retaliate. He bore injustice without striking back, because He knew the Father would vindicate Him. Jesus stood firm—not with clever argument, but with the strength of His identity.

This doesn't mean we never speak up or stand for what's right. But it does mean we don't need to fight every fight. And when we do speak, it isn't in anger—but with gentleness, humility, and wisdom (James 3:17).

Not every provocation deserves a reply. So the next time you're tempted to jump into the fray, remember the old saying: *"Never wrestle with a pig. You'll both get dirty—and the pig enjoys it."*

That proverb isn't about labeling people—it's about guarding your heart. You were made for peace, not petty fights.

You don't have to prove your point. You don't have to win the argument. You don't even have to defend yourself. Jesus has already won the battle. He is your honor, your help, your hope—and He has the final word.

Sometimes, the most upright and Godly response… is no response.

Called with a Purpose

Can God Trust You?

Because of the miraculous signs Jesus did in Jerusalem at the Passover celebration, many began to trust in him. But Jesus didn't trust them, because he knew all about people. No one needed to tell him about human nature, for he knew what was in each person's heart.
—John 2:23-25, NLT

I spent eight years serving as an administrator at an international Christian school in South Korea. It was a school with deep missional roots, committed to academic excellence and faithful in pointing students to Christ.

Three years into our time there, something unexpected happened. The Head of School called me into his office and, to my surprise, offered me the job of Assistant Head of School—the number two position in the organization.

I was humbled and honored. It was a tremendous opportunity. Yes, I had administrative experience, but that wasn't why I was offered the job. It wasn't about skills or qualifications. The Head of School said it was about trust. He trusted me to steward the school's mission and champion its vision with integrity.

Trust is a gift — a sacred responsibility.

John tells us that many trusted in Jesus because of the miracles they saw, but Jesus did not entrust Himself to them. Why? Because He knew their hearts. Their faith was based on spectacle, not surrender.

And here's the question: Can God trust you and me?

It's one thing to trust God to meet our needs. It's another to let Him trust us with His mission. That kind of trust is built day by day — in ordinary obedience, in choosing purity, and in aligning our hearts with Him through the Spirit.

Paul writes: *"If you keep yourself pure, you will be a special utensil for honorable use. Your life will be clean, and you will be ready for the Master to use you for every good work"* (2 Timothy 2:21, NLT).

We can't earn salvation, but we can be ready. Ready for God to use us. Ready for Him to trust us with opportunities that further His Kingdom.

So—can God trust you?
Lean into Jesus. Keep your heart clean. And be available.

Then watch for the doors to open.

Default or Design?

Years ago, when I was teaching fifth grade, one of my students showed up with a set of three juggling balls. She said she had won them at a carnival and wanted to donate them to the classroom. I asked why she didn't want to keep them, and she shrugged and said, "Because I don't know how to juggle."

She handed me the balls, and I started juggling. The class was wide-eyed.

"How did you learn how to do that?" they asked.

I told them the truth: I learned when I was their age. One Saturday morning I grabbed three of my dad's racquetballs, stepped away from the TV—and the voice in my head that said, *you can't*—and spent the whole day learning.

I must have bent over a thousand times to pick up dropped balls — failing, crying, getting frustrated — but by the end of the day ... I could juggle.

I told the kids, "You can either live by default or by design."

Default is staying the way you are, letting life just happen, ending up wherever you end up.

Design is taking action, choosing your way, engaging in becoming the kind of person who can juggle, write, draw, play music, invent, create beauty, help others — whatever God has put in your heart to do.

Romans 12:1–2 puts it this way:

> *So here's what I want you to do, God helping you: Take your everyday, ordinary life — your sleeping, eating, going-to-work, and walking-around life — and place it before God as an offering. Embracing what God does for you is the best thing you can do for him. Don't become so well-adjusted to your culture that you fit into it without even thinking. Instead, fix your attention on God. You'll be changed from the inside out. Readily recognize what he wants from you, and quickly respond to it. Unlike the culture around you, always dragging you down to its level of immaturity, God brings the best out of you, develops well-formed maturity in you.* (MSG)

Default says, it is what it is.
Design says, make it, move it, change it, create it.

Paul reminds us that we design our lives by fixing our eyes on Jesus and offering our whole selves — body, mind, heart, and soul — to God.

Jesus died for our sins and rose from the grave to give us abundant life — today and forever. He says to each of us, "Come to me and truly live."

Every morning, His mercies are new, and He graciously hands us three juggling balls and a Saturday and says ... start becoming.

So, are you living by default or by His design?

(By the way, that little girl decided to keep the juggling balls — and last I heard, she's getting pretty good.)

Choices Matter

The godly walk with integrity: blessed are their children who follow them.
—Proverbs 20:7, NLT

In the margin next to Proverbs 20:7, I drew an arrow that leads from the verse to my own handwritten phrase: "choices matter." (Yes, I write in my Bible!)

Life is challenging and I need wisdom, so each day, as a part of my daily Bible reading, I read a chapter out of the book of Proverbs. Years ago I learned that Billy Graham read a chapter a day out of Proverbs, and I thought it wise to follow his lead.

Every morning I know the exact chapter I will turn to—I just look at the calendar. There are thirty-one chapters in Proverbs and there are no more than thirty-one days in a month, so I check the date and then read the corresponding chapter. The result is always help and wisdom for my day.

Wisdom comes from God. It is the good, guiding, life-giving way to act, think, and live. It is God's mind and the Holy Spirit's prompting in our being and doing. It's the way to live well, appreciate what matters most, and take nothing for granted—it's the way of blessing.

God gets my attention in Proverbs 20:7 by mentioning my children, and He reminds me that my choices matter. None of us control much of what happens in this crazy world we live in, but we all get the power to choose how we "walk," think, act, talk, spend our time, and live life.

Jesus is interested in our lives—so much so that He gave His life upon the cross to save us from our sins. He wants good for His children as we walk this journey of life. He gives us help along the way, and it doesn't come from a fortune cookie—it comes from the Word of God and the Holy Spirit.

Jesus gives us wisdom. And because He is love—He gives us choice.

Choices matter.

Take Action

A father is a man that has two or more souls to save or lose.
—Austin O'Malley

That line stops me in my tracks.

It speaks to the weight of influence that a father carries—not just over his own soul, but over the souls entrusted to him. His children. His household. His legacy.

But it's not just fathers. Every one of us carries influence. Every life touches others. Whether you're a parent, a teacher, a spouse, a mentor, or a friend—someone is watching. Someone is following.

A person may think their choices are their own, that their actions and their faith are a private matter. But that's never quite true. The ripple effects of a life don't stay contained—they resonate. They shape hearts. They echo into the future—for good or for ill.

The esteemed pastor Robert Murray McCheyne once said, *"The greatest need of my people is my personal holiness."* I believe the greatest need of a home, a friendship, a community—is the same. We need people who are holy. Not perfect, but earnest. Not proud, but humble. People willing to pause and reflect, to examine their lives—to grow, to lead, and to become who God is calling them to be.

When I was fourteen, my dad woke me up one Sunday morning and said, "Get up—we're going to church." It came out of nowhere. We weren't a churchgoing family. But that morning, my dad, my mom, and my sister went to church—and I went with them.

That decision changed my life. My parents gave their lives to Jesus Christ, and a few months later, so did I. That was over forty years ago, and Jesus has been my King, my help, and my portion ever since (Psalm 119:57–58).

Not long ago, I asked my dad what led him to get us all up that Sunday morning and take us to church. He said,

> "It hit me—you were heading into high school, and I realized I only had a few years left with you under my roof. And I had failed to give you the most important thing in life. Your mom and I weren't living for the Lord, but deep down, I knew better. I knew—from the faith of my mother and grandmother—that God was what mattered most. So, we went to church."

My dad thought about it and he ***took action***. He turned to God, and it changed everything.

That's what happened to the Prodigal Son. Broken and starving in a pigpen, he came to his senses, remembered his good father, got up, and went home (Luke 15:17).

That's what happened to Zacchaeus. He climbed a tree to see Jesus—but Jesus saw him first, locked eyes with him, and called him by name. Zacchaeus responded—and became a new creation (Luke 19:1–10).

And then there's God the Father. He saw the brokenness of His children. He made a choice and sent His Son to die on a cross for the world. And it changed everything.

A holy life—and holy choices—matter. Immensely.

Joshua put it plainly: *"Choose this day whom you will serve"* (Joshua 24:15, ESV).

The moment you choose to reflect and turn toward God doesn't just shape your story—it shapes the stories of those around you. My dad made one decision. And it saved my life. The choice you make today may rescue more than just your own soul.

Look to Jesus and … ***take action.***

Are You Water or Wine?

The wine supply ran out during the festivities…
—John 2:3, NLT

Jesus' first miracle was turning water into wine. That wasn't random—it meant something.

I used to teach fifth graders the difference between living and non-living things. It sounds simple—until it isn't. Without getting too deep into the weeds, we'd define the difference like this: living things can sustain and reproduce life. Non-living things can't.

Then we'd start sorting examples.
Trees, animals, humans, bacteria, mushrooms—living.
Rocks, air, their desk, pencil, and plastic water bottle—non-living.

And then we'd get to water… and things would get murky. I'd explain that water is non-living. And without fail, my students would push back: "But water moves! Fish live in it! It helps plants grow! It's so important for life!"

And they're right—water is essential for life. But it isn't alive.

Water is a simple, inorganic compound—just hydrogen and oxygen. No carbon chains. No cells. No metabolism. No life processes. It doesn't grow, reproduce, or change on its own. It can hold life, but it doesn't possess life.

Wine, on the other hand, is the result of fermentation. It's made through a living process—one that uses microscopic, living organisms called yeast to convert sugar into alcohol and carbon dioxide. The liquid literally changes at the molecular level and it becomes something new. Wine is organic. Complex. Alive.

And for Jesus' first miracle, He turned water into wine.

He didn't just add flavor or sparkle to the liquid in those water jars. He didn't drop in some electrolytes or mix up a batch of ancient Kool-Aid. No—He turned what was non-living into something living. He took what was dead and made it alive. It was more than hospitality. It was resurrection. It was a miracle—and a metaphor. That's what Jesus does.

The wine shortage at the wedding in Cana wasn't just a party problem. It was a sign—a glimpse of the Gospel and the Kingdom to come. Where Jesus is present, lifeless things don't stay that way.

The wedding celebration was about to fall flat, and Mary, Jesus' mother, nudged Him to do something. She knew who He really was. He told her His time hadn't come.

But then… it did. And Mary told the servants: "Do whatever He tells you."

They followed His instructions—fill the jars with water, draw some out, take it to the master of ceremonies—and somewhere in the midst of their obedience, the miracle happened. The water became wine. The dead became living. That's the way the Kingdom works.

Paul says in Ephesians 2:1: *"You were dead in your trespasses and sins"* (CSB).

We all start there. Like water, we are moving, present, even helpful—but frankly, dead. And then Jesus steps in—not just to improve us, but to transform us. Not to give us a better version of ourselves, but to make us alive.

Are you water or wine? Let Jesus do His work in you. Listen for His voice. Do what He says.

And watch the miracle unfold.

Salt and ~~Fight~~… Light

You are the salt of the earth… You are the light of the world…
—Matthew 5:13–14, NIV

Yesterday morning, I was pulling onto a busy road when I felt a nudge—literally. The car behind me bumped mine. I put my car in park and got out to check. No damage. The woman behind me stepped out of her vehicle, flustered and apologetic.

"I'm so sorry," she said. "I'm just really stressed. I was distracted… I know that's not an excuse."

We talked for a moment. Nothing dramatic—just honest words exchanged between strangers. As we wrapped up, she said, "Thank you for being patient… and so kind."

That word stuck with me: ***kind.***
She said it twice—like it surprised her. And maybe it did.

Kindness isn't loud or flashy. It's not a hot take or a fight to win. It's quiet, faith-filled, and steady. And it stands out—especially in a world spoiling for a fight.

We're living in a time when everyone seems on edge. Every conversation feels like a potential argument—about politics, church, traffic… even life itself. We're braced for battle everywhere we go. All it took was a bumper-to-bumper thump to remind me how tightly wound we've all become—and how rare gentleness feels.

But Jesus calls us to something different. Listen to what He says in Matthew 5—not broken into sound bites, but as a continuous invitation and calling:

> *"Blessed are you when people insult you, persecute you and falsely say all kinds of evil against you because of me. Rejoice and be glad, because great is your reward in heaven, for in the same way they persecuted the prophets who were before you. You are the salt of the earth… You are the light of the world…"* (Matthew 5:11–14, NIV)

Did you catch that? Rejoice and be glad doesn't come after the storm—it comes in the middle of it. Right in the midst of the bumps, bruises, persecution, insults, frustrations, and false accusations. That's the context for salt and light.

We tend to break those verses into categories—pain over here, purpose over there. But Jesus wove them together. And He flipped everything.

We think the good life means having things go our way, living in comfort, moving with convenience, and staying in control. But Jesus says if you're truly following Him, you may face bumps, difficulty, and resistance—and that's where your witness matters most.

Salt doesn't shout. It doesn't post angry rebuttals. It seeps in quietly. It preserves what's good. At times it may sting a little—but it also heals.

To have that kind of quiet influence, we need wisdom—not the world's kind, but the kind that comes from above. James (the brother of Jesus) said it like this: *"The wisdom from above is first of all pure, peace-loving, gentle at all times, and willing to yield to others"* (James 3:17, NLT).

Godly wisdom doesn't clamor for attention. It works quietly, often unnoticed.

As E. Stanley Jones put it: *"We are to be salt before we can be light. No man can shine in obviousness unless he is willing to permeate in obscurity."*

Obscurity. Insults. Weakness. They don't mean you're doing it wrong. They might mean you're right where you're supposed to be.

Look to Jesus and listen to His words. Let them steady you. Stay faithful. And when the world is itching for a fight—be kind. Because it's not about the fight.

It's about the light.

God's Greatest Sign and Wonder...Is You

Jesus once told His disciples, "Do not rejoice that the spirits submit to you, but rejoice that your names are written in heaven."
—Luke 10:20, NIV

We're drawn to the spectacular—big stories, miracles, and testimonies that move us to tears. We long for worship experiences that give us goosebumps and prophetic words that stir our hearts. None of that is wrong. Much of it is good and beautiful. Signs and wonders are real—they stir faith, awaken awe, grab our attention, and glorify God. But here's the truth: they're never the point.

We live in a time—and a Christian culture—where power is treated as proof. The bigger the miracle, the more "spiritual" it feels. And while we rightly celebrate when God moves, Jesus never meant for our faith to rest on the dramatic.

When the seventy-two disciples returned from their mission, they were buzzing with excitement. God had moved through them. They had spoken with authority, healed the sick, and cast out evil in Jesus' name. "Even the demons submit to us!" they said.

But Jesus gently redirected them. He affirmed what had happened—yet pointed them to something greater: *"Do not rejoice that the spirits submit to you, but rejoice that your names are written in heaven."*

In other words: Joy isn't in what you can do—it's in whose you are.

Paul understood this. To believers in Rome—people he hadn't even met yet—he wrote, *"I long to see you so that I may impart to you some spiritual gift to make you strong—that is, that you and I may be mutually encouraged by each other's faith"* (Romans 1:11–12, NIV).

The *"spiritual gift"* Paul longed to give wasn't a dramatic display of power or a one-time miracle. It wasn't even a message. It was his presence—offered in faith.

The gift was the steady, Spirit-filled encouragement that comes through shared life, mutual trust, prayer, and love. In short, it was his walk with Jesus lived openly among them.

And that's often how the Spirit works—not in spectacle, but in steady faith. Not only in signs, but in the slow, faithful work of love. The miracle isn't always on a stage or in a church service. More often, it's in how we show up—in our homes, workplaces, and everyday relationships.

The most Spirit-filled gift we offer isn't a word of prophecy or healing—it's our life, offered in love, shaped by Jesus, and shared with one another.

In Acts 1:8, Jesus calls us His "witnesses"—those who carry His presence and speak His truth in the world. And in 2 Corinthians 5:20, the Apostle Paul says we are "ambassadors"—representatives of Christ, entrusted with His message as though God Himself were speaking through us.

That's not just metaphor—it's a mission.

The Lord uses signs and wonders to bless His people and bring glory to Himself. They are good and beautiful. They stir faith, awaken awe, and honor God.

But the greatest witness to the world isn't a stage, a platform, or a miraculous moment. It's an ordinary, faithful life—a living, breathing,

Jesus-shaped, Spirit-filled person who is humble, kind, courageous, and loving.

The world may crave spectacle. But in God's economy, the greatest sign and wonder… is you.

See Others Rightly

One of the greatest mistakes in the world is to tell yourself what a man is like; you do not know what he is like. The only One who can teach you how to deal with the various specimens around you is the Holy Spirit. —Oswald Chambers

I've spent a lot of my life around people—in classrooms, committee meetings, boardrooms, churches, and living rooms, both in the States and overseas. You'd think that after so many meetings, meals, and moments with people—from Idaho to Indonesia—I'd be better at knowing how to love them well. But the truth is, I still get it wrong more than I'd like to admit.

Some folks are easy to love. Others? Not so much. They're draining. Difficult. Sometimes even deceptive. I've picked up a few instincts over the years—how to read a room, spot a red flag, or protect myself when needed. I used to call that wisdom. Sometimes it probably was. But often it was just guardedness dressed up in church clothes.

We live in a world that normalizes suspicion and applauds cynicism. We scroll past headlines, posts, and comments that make it easy to write people off before hearing their story. And without even realizing it, I've learned to do the same. I told myself I was just being careful—discerning. But in the process, I stopped being compassionate. I labeled people in my mind before I looked them in the eye.

Jesus didn't do that.

He saw the heart. He knew what people were really like—but He didn't turn away. He engaged with love. He never sidestepped the truth, and He didn't shut down when things got messy. He stayed open, even when it hurt. That kind of love is foreign in a world like ours.

And honestly? I don't know how to do that—not on my own. I want to protect myself. I want to be safe. I want to be right. But the Spirit keeps whispering, "Let Me show you another way."

And so, I'm slowly and imperfectly learning that discernment doesn't have to be defensive. That wisdom can still be warm. That the Holy Spirit sees more than I ever will—and can teach me to see people not just for who they appear to be, but for who they really are… and who they're becoming.

"Man looks at the outward appearance, but the Lord looks at the heart" (1 Samuel 16:7, ESV).

I want to see others like that—like Jesus does. I want to trust the Spirit to show me how.

This world pulls us toward judgment—snap decisions, sharp edges, and guarded hearts. But the call of Christ is different: to love God and to love your neighbor. The two are bound together. Which means when I close my heart to people, I'm also closing my heart to God.

I need help.

"The wisdom from above is first of all pure. It is also peace-loving, gentle at all times, and willing to yield to others" (James 3:17, NLT).

That's the wisdom I want. That's the posture I need to take.

Holy Spirit, help me to see others rightly.

Hope on the Horizon

A Tale of Two Rivers

When a dirty river and a clean river come together, the result is—dirty river.
—William Stafford

There I saw a stream flowing east from beneath the door of the Temple … The waters of this stream will make the salty waters of the Dead Sea fresh and pure. … Life will flourish wherever this water flows.
—Ezekiel 47:1, 8-9, NLT

In this tale of two rivers, Stafford speaks a hard truth. We're up to our necks in murky water. Life in this world, where negativity is the norm and decay is the default, is hard. The pollution of global conflict, never-ending news, relentless fear, and the sludge of social media swirl around us, and the result is—dirty river

But God's river is different. Ezekiel speaks of the Truth—a river that doesn't become tainted, but transforms. Flowing from His Holy Temple, it touches the barren, the lifeless, the polluted, and makes them new. God's river grows deeper, stronger, and purer as it flows, bringing healing, restoration, and life. When the stream from the Temple meets the Dead Sea, the result is—clean river.

This river of life isn't just a vision—it's a reality—and His name is Jesus. *"Whoever believes in me, as Scripture has said, rivers of living water will flow from within them"* (John 7:38, NIV).

When we look to and follow Christ, His Spirit flows in us and through us, and it doesn't just cleanse—it transforms. No matter how "murky" things may be, His water saves, sanctifies, and gives life.

In this tale of two rivers—dirty or clean—where do you find yourself?

In the midst of hard truth or… the Truth?

Looking to Jesus

Let us run with endurance the race that is set before us, looking to Jesus.
—Hebrews 12:1–2, ESV

The other day I pulled out a stack of my old journals—1998 through 2006—looking for some details for a friend. Before I knew it, I was lost in the pages. Each entry took me back: to people and places, celebrations and setbacks, laughter and tears.

I found forgotten hopes, old questions, and prayers I hadn't read in years. And through it all, one thing stood out: God's faithfulness and help.

Those eight years were full of global uncertainty and personal change—Y2K, 9/11, my kids starting school, and several career shifts. I made choices, took steps, and walked through moments—some wise, some not so wise—that shaped my journey. But looking back now, I can see what I couldn't then: I wasn't the one writing the whole story.

Jeremiah's words ring true, *"I know, Lord, that our lives are not our own. We are not able to plan our own course"* (Jeremiah 10:23, NLT).

My journals are more than records of events—they capture what was happening in my heart. Again and again, I wrote prayers like, "Jesus, guide me," "Jesus, show me," "Jesus, help me." I didn't have all the answers, but I did what I could—I looked to Jesus.

And I still do.

The world is unsteady. Life will shift—relationships, finances, health. The future is unknown, and the pages are blank.

So I do the one thing I can: I fix my gaze on Jesus. I step forward, trusting Him with the story. And one day, when I look back at my journals, I know I'll see it again—God's faithfulness and help—written across the pages of my life.

Looking to Jesus.

Before Honor

The fear of the Lord is instruction in wisdom, and humility comes before honor.
—Proverbs 15:33, ESV

In life we all face situations—and people—that feel impossible. A marriage frozen in years of tension. A fractured friendship that never healed. A blow-up at work that left scars. And now we're stuck.

What do you do when there are no good answers? Something has to change—and usually, we want it to be… them.

I often meet with people searching for answers. And the counsel I give is both simple and hard: you can't change someone else. The only person you can change is… you.

When it comes to conflict, the world offers only two options: fight harder or walk away. But Scripture points to a better way—the one that leaves space for God's hand to break in.

It's humility.

It sounds upside down, because it is. Humility isn't pretty, and it rarely feels noble. It looks like swallowing your pride and saying the hardest words in the world: "I was wrong. I'm sorry. Please forgive me." It looks like apologizing without excuses, letting go of self-justification, opening your hands, and trusting God with the outcome."

Here's the mystery: when we go low, God shows up. In Proverbs 15:33, the Hebrew word for "honor" is ***kabod***—substance, dignity, glory. It's the same word often used for God's presence, His nearness pressing heavy among His people. And that's what we long for when we're stuck in the impossible—that His presence would press into the mess and do what we cannot.

So how does this happen? Proverbs makes the order clear: *humility comes before honor.* God's glory doesn't rest on pride—it comes only through contrition. That's the same pattern God gave His people in 2 Chronicles 7:14: *"If my people, who are called by my name, will humble themselves and pray and seek my face and turn from their wicked ways, then I will hear from heaven, and I will forgive their sin and will heal their land"* (NIV).

What is your land? Could it be your marriage? Your family? Your friendships? Your workplace? These are the fields where pride scorches the soil, but humility waters it again.

Healing comes when we stop demanding our way and start walking God's way—when we humble ourselves, turn, and pray. His glory doesn't just heal nations—it heals homes. It heals relationships. It heals the ground right under our feet.

This is the way of Jesus. Philippians 2 tells us He *"humbled himself"* all the way to the cross. He went low—bearing what He didn't owe, carrying what wasn't His fault—so that God's saving power could break through our impossible. And then Paul says, *"God exalted him to the highest place."*

God's honor was displayed in Jesus' life, and James reminds us He will do the same for you and me: *"Humble yourselves before the Lord, and he will lift you up"* (James 4:10, NIV).

Maybe you're facing something—or someone—you just can't fix. You don't know how to move forward. You're out of words and out of answers. Good. That's where God's glory does its best work.

The way of wisdom says: follow Jesus—go low in the situation and before the person in front of you. Trust Him with the miracle.

Because, before honor—before the breakthrough, before the healing, before God's glory breaks in—comes humility.

Not Alone

Be sure of this: I am with you always, even to the end of the age.
—Matthew 28:20, NLT

Do you feel alone sometimes? Me too.

Most major news outlets, many health care providers, the Surgeon General and (of course) Google, all say that the new epidemic in the U.S. is loneliness. But you and I know this is not a "new" problem; it's an age-old problem that just keeps resurfacing.

Even in the best of circumstances, we all experience the sense of being alone. For me, it shows up when I face situations where I don't know what to do. Whether it's the big challenges and struggles of life or just the little hiccups, hurts, and hurdles of the day, the feeling that creeps in—though I don't dare say it out loud—is, "I am alone."

Just the other day I was frustrated to find my roof leaking—again. I thought I had it fixed! Now what do I do? Who do I call? How much is this going to cost? And as the rain fell, I was drenched in loneliness.

A few years ago, I faced a critical illness that had all the doctors stumped. My body, mind, and life were ebbing away, and I was desperate. The medical professionals were working hard for me, my family was loving me, my friends were supporting me, and countless people around the world were praying for me… and still I felt alone.

There is no rhyme or reason to loneliness. It comes when we are by ourselves, and it ambushes us in a crowd. It can hit us when life is hard, and sometimes even when everything is fine.

The Enemy of our hearts whispers the lie, "You are alone." But thanks be to God, we are not. God is with us in our confusion and suffering—and even before we step into those moments!

Jesus' last words to you and me, and to every lonely person who has ever lived, are: *"Be sure of this: I am with you always."* In God's economy, always means… ***always.***

In Joshua 5, the leader of God's people is staring at the towering walls of Jericho. I'm sure Joshua felt alone, but he wasn't. He encountered the Lord, who told him that the ground he was standing on—on the very edge of the impossible—was holy because God was already there.

In John 6, the disciples are in a storm. The wind howls, the waves rise, and fear grips their hearts. They felt helpless and alone—but they weren't. Jesus was already there—walking on the water toward them.

And Paul reminds us in Philippians 4:5-6: *"The Lord is near. Do not be anxious about anything, but in every situation, by prayer and petition, with thanksgiving, present your requests to God."*

Did you catch that? *The Lord is near.* Before the roof leaks. Before the phone rings. Before the battle begins. Before the healing happens. Before help arrives. Even before we call His name (and even if we don't) … Jesus is with us.

Loneliness is real, and it can be dark. But it doesn't get the last word. Look to Jesus with hope and take heart—because when we bring anything to Him, we are standing on holy ground.

You and I are not alone.

“Hangry” or Worse?

Michal, Saul’s daughter, was barren the rest of her life.
—2 Samuel 6:23, MSG

The night should have been special. My wife, daughters, and sons-in-law were all gathered around the table—a rare moment when our busy lives aligned, giving us the chance to laugh, talk, and simply enjoy being together. But I missed the moment.

I was physically present—sitting right there—but my heart was somewhere else. Irritation, criticism, and frustration consumed my mind. The restaurant was busy, the service slow, the waiter inattentive… and I was fuming. (I wish I could say I was just “hangry,” but I wasn’t.)

Instead of joining in the joy and beauty at the table, I quenched it. My family felt the weight of my spirit, and my attitude dampened theirs. Negativity left me empty, lifeless, barren. I let frustration dictate my presence—and in doing so, I missed the fun, beauty, blessing, and love…the real feast happening all around me.

A fretting, distracted, critical heart always results in an empty, barren life.

Michal, the wife of King David, knew something of this. She stood in the very presence of God, watching as the Ark of the Covenant was brought into Jerusalem. But instead of celebrating, she sat in judgment. As David danced before the Lord, Michal watched from a distance, her heart hardened with contempt. She could have joined the celebration—but she didn't. Consumed with irritation, criticism, frustration, and pride, she missed the moment.

The result? Barrenness—not just physical, but spiritual. She missed the joy of God's presence and the fruit-bearing abundance that comes from a surrendered heart. She was near the things of God (sitting right at the table!) but missed the fun, beauty, blessing, and love happening all around her.

There's no shortage of things in our world—and in our hearts—that stir criticism and frustration. The Enemy works tirelessly to distract us, causing us to miss the blessing even when we're sitting right in the middle of it. We can sit at the table and never taste the goodness set before us. Surrounded by worship, fellowship, and God's Spirit, we can still quench it—and walk away empty.

But there is a way back. His name is Jesus.

We must turn away from the distractions of the Enemy and *"fix our eyes on Jesus."* He is the one who said, *"In this world you will have trouble. But take heart! I have overcome the world"* (John 16:33, NIV).

Are you "hangry" or worse? Is your spirit barren? Lean into the abundant life that is Jesus. Enter the celebration. Don't miss the feast. Be present. Be life-giving.

"Taste and see that the Lord is good" (Psalm 34:8, NIV).

Forget It

Forgetting what is behind... —Philippians 3:13, NIV

My grandparents had a small farm in Southern Idaho and it was my privilege to spend my summers working alongside my grandad on that farm. It was a great adventure that included tractors, milk cows, irrigation boots, barn cats, hay bales, hard work, and two dogs—Tara and Pug.

Those two dogs knew every square inch of that 100-acre farm, and they spent their days exploring the fields, swimming in the pond, sleeping in the sun, and hunting the yellow-bellied marmot—commonly known as a rock chuck.

After lunch one day, my grandad and I walked out the back door of the house and were surprised to find a large, dead rock chuck lying on the back step. Tara and Pug stood nearby, panting, slobbering, and beaming with pride. We celebrated their triumph with pats on the head and lots of "good dogs" all around, and then my grandad told me to grab a shovel and go bury that thing in a nearby pasture.

I dragged the lifeless marmot out into the field, and the dogs followed me eagerly and attentively, brimming with joy. I dug what I thought was a deep hole and I buried the carcass. Two weeks later, the matted, stinking remains of that rock chuck appeared again on the back step of the house. Nearby, Tara and Pug lay innocently in the yard, but the traces of dirt on their front paws and noses told the story. Needless to say, I reburied the creature in a different spot, without Tara and Pug tagging along, and that was the end of that. They forgot about the rock chuck and resumed their life of fun and adventure on the farm.

Those crazy dogs had dug up that dead thing, and I understand why—they're dogs. But why do you and I do the same thing? It's been said that "memory is like a crazy woman that hoards colored rags and throws away food." We remember the things we should forget, and forget the things we should remember.

We all have junk, mistakes, regrets and sin in our lives, but the Good News is that Jesus went to the cross and took all of that dead stuff and buried it. It is gone! All we have left to do is to forget it, and live a redeemed, victorious life of adventure and joy in Jesus.

In Isaiah 43:18-19, the prophet tells us to, *"Forget the former things; do not dwell on the past. See, I am doing a new thing!"* (NIV)

In Philippians 3:13-14, the Apostle Paul tells us how he lived the victorious life, *"Forgetting what is behind and straining toward what is ahead, I press on toward the goal to win the prize for which God has called me heavenward in Christ Jesus."* (NIV)

What are you keeping that you should throw away? What are you remembering that you should be forgetting? What are you digging up that Jesus has buried by His grace? *"Where sin abounded, grace did much more abound"* (Romans 5:20, KJV).

Don't dwell on your past, your mistakes, your sin.

Forget it... and fix your eyes on Jesus.

The Best Miles

Though outwardly we are wasting away, yet inwardly we are being renewed by day.
—2 Corinthians 4:16, NIV

The Old Tire

As one of four, I carried a car;
On business of utmost import.
From summit to shore, I traveled afar;
All the while my time growing short.

I rolled along, till my tread was all spent;
Tossed away—thin, worn and unfit.
On the side of the road, to the ditch I was sent;
To die lying still in the pit.

But life ebbed again at the hand of a boy;
A push and a roll were my test.
I found all joy, in the guise of a toy;
These miles are some of my best.

I saw two boys at an orphanage in Bangalore, India, pushing an old tire they had found along the road. They didn't have soccer balls, video games, or playground equipment—but they had that tire. Around and around they went, laughing and shouting, their bare feet kicking up red dust.

I couldn't stop watching. That tire was finished—thrown to the side, discarded, worn out—but in the hands of those boys, it was reborn. Its "best miles" weren't spent carrying the weight of a car. They were spent bringing joy.

And it struck me: even while that tire was doing what it was made to do—carrying its load, being "important"—it was wearing down. Its time was growing short with every mile.

Isn't that us? We spend years doing what matters most—raising kids, serving others, building businesses, loving our neighbors—carrying the weight God has entrusted to us. And yet, even in those seasons of purpose, our strength runs down, our tread wears thin.

Sometimes I feel like that old tire. Maybe you do too. Spent. Worn down. Forgotten. There are days I wonder if my best miles are behind me—if the most valuable part of me has already been used up.

And it stirs something deep—that ache for what once was, for the strength we used to have, for the laughter and lightness of childhood. We hear that longing echoed in some of our most nostalgic lines of poetry:

> *Backward, turn backward, O time in your flight.*
> *Make me a child again just for tonight.*
> —Elizabeth Akers Allen

That longing is real—and good. It points us to something we were made for: wonder, trust, and the chance to begin again.

Jesus offers something better than turning back the clock. He says, *"Unless you turn and become like little children, you will never enter the kingdom of heaven"* (Matthew 18:3, ESV).

The Kingdom life isn't about proving we can still carry the weight of the world—it's about learning to trust, to wonder, to play again.

Even when we feel discarded, Jesus doesn't leave us in the ditch. He stoops down, picks us up, and rolls us into new life.

*Though outwardly we are wasting away, yet inwardly we are being renewed day by day (*2 Corinthians 4:16, NIV).

Maybe your "important miles" are done. Perhaps that's not a loss—maybe that's grace. The best miles aren't the ones that prove your strength, but the ones that reveal His.

Let Jesus pick you up. Let Him renew you. Let Him roll you toward joy again—because in Him, …*the best miles* are always in front of you.

Leap of Faith

I will follow you, Lord; but...
—Luke 9:61, NIV

I used to be an elementary school teacher. A few years ago, I sent out an email to let my colleagues know I'd be leaving the classroom to become an associate pastor. They were all kind, supportive, and excited for me — but inside, I was feeling the weight of the moment.

I loved teaching and working with students. I'd spent a life doing it. And there's a certain security that comes with the job—a steady paycheck, a predictable schedule, summers off, and a rhythm to the year you can set your watch by.

Walking away from all that to jump into full-time ministry? That's a leap.

Spencer worked in the cafeteria and delivered student breakfasts to the classrooms every morning before school. For a couple of years, he stopped by my room almost daily with three trays of food and a cheerful comment about sports, movies, or whatever holiday break was coming next.

One morning after he heard I was leaving, he came into my room and said, "So, you're not gonna be here next year? It's sure been great to work with you."

And then came the line that got me: "I think this decision could turn into something really great. *Sometimes you just gotta take a leap of faith.*" I laughed—not at him, but with this sense that God had just spoken to me *through* him. There was something innocent, almost ironic, about being told that I needed to take a leap of faith... into a job that is all about faith!

But Spencer was right. I was standing on the edge of a decision that scared me a bit — leaving the safety of the known for the wide-open unknown of what God was calling me to do.

In those months leading up to my first day at the church, I sensed God whispering, *I'm preparing you. I'm using everything I've taught you to get you ready for what's next. Trust Me, even when you can't see what's coming.*

Looking back now, I can see how true that was. God has been near. He's been faithful. And He's used every season of my life to prepare me for this one.

Oswald Chambers put it this way: *If you're going to do anything worthwhile, sometimes you have to risk everything and leap.*

That's what I did. And God caught me.

Serving as a pastor has been such a joy—more rewarding and fulfilling than I ever imagined.

In the Lord, the safest way forward isn't always the most secure. The life—and death—of Jesus show us that God's way can be difficult, dangerous, even costly, … but it's always good.

Maybe you're standing on the edge of something right now—a decision, a calling, a change that feels uncertain. Jesus still says, *"Follow Me."* (Matthew 4:19) And He still promises, *"I am with you always, even to the end of the age"* (Matthew 28:20, NLT).

Hebrews 11:6 reminds us that *"without faith it is impossible to please God"* (NIV).

Life was never meant to be lived playing it safe—not in a world as broken as this one. Real security comes from trusting that the guiding, sustaining arms of Jesus are strong enough to catch you and keep you.

Sometimes you just gotta take a leap of faith.

Paradise is Coming

Have I not commanded you? Be strong and courageous.
—Joshua 1:9, NIV

I started a new job not long ago, and I love it. But I've learned over time that no matter how good a situation seems, it won't be perfect. Every job, relationship, or circumstance comes with its own set of obstacles. Why? Because we live in a broken world.

As Christians, we often assume that when we step into God's will for our lives, everything should be easy. If we're obeying God, living out our faith, and walking with Jesus, shouldn't life be smooth sailing?

We need to be careful not to confuse the Promised Land with paradise.

When we think of the Promised Land, we might picture a place of rest, abundance, and fulfillment. But the biblical reality is different. The Promised Land was, "a land flowing with milk and honey," but it was also a place of challenge, struggle, and hardship. When the Israelites crossed the Jordan River, they didn't waltz into paradise—they marched into warfare.

When Joshua and Caleb finally entered the land God had promised, they found giants, walled cities, and enemies who didn't want them there. The Promised Land wasn't a retreat—it was a battlefield. And yet, it was where they were meant to be. It was the place God led them—and He promised to go before them, fight for them, and fulfill His purpose in their lives.

Too often, we confuse our calling with comfort. We assume that if God has provided and led us somewhere, the path should be smooth. We wrongly equate the "Promised Land" with paradise, and then we live in doubt, disillusionment, and sorrow when trials arise.

The truth is, paradise isn't here yet. Jesus said, *"I go to prepare a place for you"* (John 14:2, KJV). That place is Heaven, our eternal home, where every tear will be wiped away. But for now, we are pilgrims in the Promised Land.

We walk with God, but still in a broken world. We experience His promises in the midst of wrestling with life's realities. The Promised Land is where we stand in faith, trusting that He is with us through the difficulties. It's where we fight the good fight because He has called us to this place and time—and He is with us.

So, if you find yourself facing insurmountable walls, giants in the land, or rivers that seem impossible to cross, take courage. The Promised Land was never meant to be paradise; it's the place where God grows your faith, strengthens your trust, and uses you for His glory.

Press on: look to Jesus, keep walking, keep trusting, and remember...

Paradise is coming.

Gentle Whispers, Holy Reminders

Draw near to God, and he will draw near to you.
—James 4:8, ESV—

If you've made it this far—thank you. It has been a joy to walk with you through these seventy-seven *Nudgings*. My prayer is that one of these gentle whispers blessed your heart, turned your eyes toward Jesus, and reminded you that He is near.

"Paradise is coming" was the last word of this book — but the journey isn't over. Each day is another chance to know God more, listen for His Spirit, and walk in faith.

If a Nudging spoke to you, please tell someone. Share it with a friend, start a conversation, or pass this book along. I believe God nudged me to share these thoughts with others, and He loves to use ordinary people and everyday moments to spread His good news.

This *first edition* is just the beginning of a journey I hope we'll keep walking together.

Please sign up for free weekly Nudgings at hsnudgings.com. And if this book blessed you, consider leaving a review where you purchased it — your words might be the very nudge someone else needs to take a step toward Jesus.

Draw near to God. Stay in the Word. Keep praying. And above all, keep looking to Jesus.

Press on,
Ryan

Acknowledgements

This book is not the work of one person. It is the fruit of many prayers, many conversations, and many holy nudges along the way — and I am deeply grateful.

To my family—my precious wife, Dina, who faithfully read every Nudging before I sent it into the world; my daughters, whose likes and loves on social media meant more than they know; and my parents, who still think every new Nudging is "the best one yet"—thank you all for your love, patience, and constant encouragement.

To my church family at Eagle Naz—thank you for giving me the gift of living out these reflections in community and for allowing me to share them with you each week. Your encouragement kept me writing.

To Pastor Jerry, my "biggest fan," I so appreciate your kind words. And to friends and readers who believed in me and prayed for me — your support carried me further than you know.

I'm grateful to Isaiah Guerrero, whose creativity shaped this book's beautiful cover and website—and whose friendship is a gift. And to every reader who nudged me to keep writing, thank you. This book belongs to you as much as to me.

Above all, I thank Jesus—the source and the reason for every gentle whisper, every holy reminder, every... ***nudge of His Spirit.***

About the Author

Ryan M. Roberts has spent more than three decades living at the intersection of faith, education, and everyday life. He serves as Associate Pastor at Eagle Nazarene Church in Eagle, Idaho, where he leads, encourages, preaches, teaches, mentors, serves, prays, and walks alongside people in their journey with Jesus.

An ordained elder in the Church of the Nazarene since 2003, Ryan holds a Doctor of Ministry in 21st Century Christian Leadership (Drew University), a Master of Arts in Spiritual Formation, and a Master of Education in Curriculum and Instruction.

In addition to pastoral ministry, Ryan has served as a university professor, school principal, international Christian school administrator, and longtime public-school educator.

Ryan has been married to his wife, Dina, for 37 years. He is the proud father of two grown daughters, father-in-law to two wonderful sons, and "Grandad" to one beloved granddaughter.

If you asked Ryan what matters most, he would tell you this: **Jesus loves you and wants to give you the abundant life that is only found in Him. There is no greater thing.**

Whether in the pulpit, the classroom, or through his writing, Ryan's passion is simple: helping people hear and respond to the gentle voice of Jesus in the ordinary moments of life. You can connect with Ryan and sign up for weekly Nudgings at hsnudgings.com.

Made in the USA
Coppell, TX
18 February 2026

71778858R00132